WE'RE PUT HERE TO LOVE

A Memoir with Poems

JANET W. BICKEL

I dedicate this book to my mom, Jean Finley Wetzel, my first source of love and best source of inspiration.

"And we are put on earth a little space / that we may learn to bear the beams of love."—William Blake

CONTENTS

PART I

ORIGINS

I am my grandparents and parents' continued minds and genes. Anything good that we are given—once we notice it—is ours forever.

FAMILY TREE

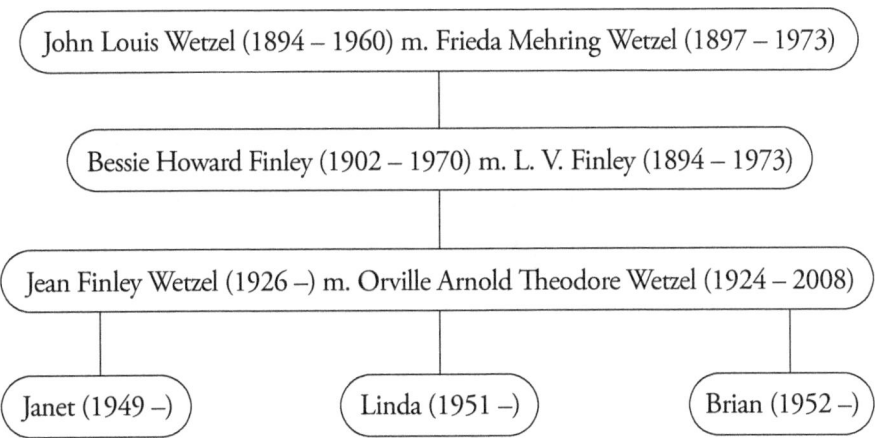

John Louis Wetzel (1894 – 1960) m. Frieda Mehring Wetzel (1897 – 1973)

Bessie Howard Finley (1902 – 1970) m. L. V. Finley (1894 – 1973)

Jean Finley Wetzel (1926 –) m. Orville Arnold Theodore Wetzel (1924 – 2008)

Janet (1949 –)   Linda (1951 –)   Brian (1952 –)

CHAPTER 1

GRANDPARENTS

My parents both grew up in Red Bud, Illinois, a little farming town an hour southeast of St. Louis, Missouri, that we visited frequently during my childhood.

JOHN LOUIS WETZEL (1894–1960) (66 YEARS)

Unconscious of the thumb lodged in my mouth, I am yet so innocent that, when Granpa Wetzel calls me, saying, "Let's see that thumb of yours," I actually walk toward him. He lunges at me, blade in hand. "I'm gonna cut that thing right off." This terrifying event is the only time I ever remember him laughing.

A father of eight, with money tight, Granpa Wetzel suffers a back injury on a construction job and after that finds only temporary work. He must've been in pain most of the time, except when he was drinking. The family survives on their garden and on his hunting and river fishing. Once Granpa orders my sister and me pulled from bed to photograph us inches from the monstrous, smelly catfish he's just caught.

Most of his seven sons acquire hunting and butchering skills, and the butcher-block table in the back sees the blood of hundreds of deer, squirrels, rabbits, ducks, geese, turkeys, fish, snapping turtles, and sides of hog and beef.

One summer noon Granma and I are alone in her kitchen when, suddenly shrieking, she rushes outside. Granpa is reeling down the street, singing at the top of his lungs. A few years later on Christmas Eve, accepting cheer at a tavern after serving as the town Santa (he looks the part), he slips and cracks open his skull on the bathtub.

FRIEDA MEHRING WETZEL (1897–1973) (76 YEARS)

Second oldest of nine surviving siblings, Frieda grows up speaking German and working the fields. Frieda gives birth to Elmer, Henry, Ralph, Orville (my dad), Bernice, Eric, John Jr., and Harry. All seven sons serve in the armed forces, with WWII killing Ralph, the most academically and athletically promising one.

On Saturday mornings, by the time my family arrives in Red Bud, her kitchen is a heaven of freshly baked bread, coffee cakes, and pies. Granma Wetzel's geranium-scented winter cellar brims with her canned preserves, peaches, white Queen Anne cherries, pickles, and tender beef. Every dish she puts on the table is delicious (fresh lard was the secret). No matter how many she's serving, she never seems rushed or ill-tempered, nor is she the slightest bit impressed with herself.

Granma Wetzel is the first to put a coin in my hand and trust me with an errand to a store. The creamery sells the smoothest, richest cottage cheese, just the right complement to her pork sausage and fried potatoes and onions. Frieda Wetzel is also renowned for her quilting and sewing. She rarely sits down without some handwork in her lap. Her commodious lap is the only one I have a memory of. Her apron pocket contains Juicy Fruit gum—I'm hooked.

In her garden she teaches me to dig a potato, wash it at the well, and bite right in—fabulous (impressing younger cousins who can't imagine eating a potato raw). She points out hummingbirds, surprise lilies (the stalks grow inches overnight), and snapdragons that accept my fingertip. She's so proud of her plants that even in her seventies, she stays up well past her bedtime to witness her night-blooming Star of Bethlehem cactus. Her hands are rough and nails are dirt-stained—more interesting than other women's hands.

One perfect summer morning, dressed in a new blue sleeveless dress decorated with flat bows on the shoulders, I shine with happiness to be walking alone with her to church. I feel very special as she proudly introduces me to her friends: "Here is Orville's oldest."

Granma endures a mastectomy, after which she is never free from pain; she eventually dies of cancer that had spread. What a Friend she had in Jesus—her favorite hymn, which I was fortunate to get to play on the piano and sing for her. While she never speaks of it, her faith carries her through all the trials and losses in her life, including the loss of many of her beloved brothers and sisters.

A letter to me: "I will drop you a few lines, got yours a while back, we had awful hot weather here and so dry had a nice shower Sunday but need more if we want corn so hope it rains more soon so that farmers get something, its bad the poor stock don't have a pasture to graze, and I only did quilting, have to sit in by the fan anyway so I might as well quilt don't have that much sewing and no canning have to do something cant just sit around thinking, I had the shingles its breaking out on your body across my ribs and was so hot couldn't have no cloths on it. Hope to see you soon, try and make it here. I got klump [my favorite sausage] saved." And her last note: "Thanks my Dear Janet, for the nice card, and what it really means to me, even you so far away there thinking of me."

Her death hits me with primal force.

My First Seeds

Holy week and kneeling
    palms cup seeds of sugar snaps and lettuces and beans—
    my first bed of vegetables
    and longed for like a journey home.
Patpatpatpatpat
    hands press in with love—
    these seeds all but invisible
    as love can be.
My mental cellar's full already—
    not just to crunch between my teeth
    and to serve others—my granma reincarnate—
    also as experiment gone well and edible.
Chill wind, mad thunder
    laugh me back indoors—
    receipts and broken nails tell more the story—
    humbling me as if I needed more.

BESSIE HOWARD FINLEY (1902–1970) (68 YEARS)

A farm girl who manages to graduate from high school, Bessie births Howard, then three years later Jean, then twelve years later John. She plays piano at her church and at a prison's services (an hour bus ride away), and is an untiring hospital volunteer, visitor of the down-on-their-luck, and "Worthy Matron" (the highest authority within chapters of the Order of the Eastern Star).

Most importantly to me, she is also town librarian. In that one room in city hall adjacent to the jail, I spend many of the happiest (and the first heavenly air-conditioned) hours of my girlhood discovering Frank Baum's Oz books and later poring over *American Girl* magazine.

Many summers my sister Linda and I get a blessed week in Red Bud. Granma Finley introduces us to her friends and spoils us, buying our favorite cookies and, best of all, giving us our bath and covering us with talc—the luxury!

Because they buy us presents, we assume that Granpa Finley is rich, only later learning that they own nothing but a car and their furniture, which includes a piano on which Granma improvises accompaniment for any popular tune or hymn. Her tiny kitchen produces wonders like homemade noodles with pot roast gravy.

She always looks put together, often in blue print shirtwaists. Linda and I get to play with her perfume bottles—Avon and Emeraude—and costume jewelry. Her neat appearance belies unspoken suffering. Once after being attacked in the basement of their building by an acquaintance, she lied to Granpa about her bruises, or there would've been violence. Mom later tells me that Granma felt intensely the constrictions of her lack of education and decades-long fear of another pregnancy.

As kind as she is to me, I'm wary of her judgmental eye. Once when I am about three, she greets me with "That thumb is going to ruin your face." In revenge I crayon the freshly wallpapered hall she had been showing my parents, hide behind a door, and don't remember what happened next, which probably means that I felt sufficiently loved. But I never stop feeling observed. Granpa might've felt this way too—they bicker a lot.

One stifling summer morning when Granpa and Granma are visiting us in Rock Hill, she is peeling peaches when she has a heart attack.

After that, climbing the two very long flights of stairs to their apartment is hard, and a year later congestive heart failure sets in. She dies only a few months shy of my wedding, which she'd so generously welcomed, filling a cedar chest with dishes and embroidered pillowcases. On my last visit to her in the hospital, I wear a skirt she'd made for me, which I've drastically shortened to expose my black fishnet-hosed legs. She's horrified. What a typically thoughtless twenty-year-old I am, with no way to communicate the depth of my love for her.

L. V. FINLEY (1894–1973) (79 YEARS)

Inexplicably christened Leah Vivian and known most of his life as LV, Granpa Finley serves in France during WWI for only a few months before taking a bullet in the collarbone (a few inches lower and I wouldn't exist). A letter he wrote from the hospital in France states: "I've had enough; have had a million dollars' worth of experience but wouldn't give five cents for another million dollars' worth." During WWII he joins the Seabees, where he develops a low opinion of the officers.

Nothing could dent his patriotism, however, and he teaches his grandkids how to honor the flag and to appreciate marching bands. That our national anthem can even now swell my heart is thanks to him.

During the Depression and beyond, a suitable teaching job is hard to come by. The extent of his talents is not apparent until his years as Red Bud High School's principal and science and math teacher, and happiest of all—band leader and track coach.

On retirement, he devotes himself to improving the city park, beginning with planting hundreds of trees and mapping the old city cemetery. He crafts models of a fort, picnic shelters, and a kinderplatz that his grandkids can play with, and then he builds the actual structures. He leads a fund-raising campaign for a swimming pool, going so far as to appear on the high school stage in a woman's dress with a mop for a wig. This pool is heaven to Brian, Linda, and me, since otherwise we have no access to one.

Granpa whistles and sings while he works—a favorite: "Lazy bones sleepin' in the sun, how ya gonna get your day's work done?" His enthusiasm for all food is infectious. ("By golly, doesn't that smell good!") After the big dinner at noon, he extends his long body on the floor, with his head under the table for a short nap. He models excellent posture and encourages the then unusual practice of taking a walk after Sunday and holiday dinners.

His challenging side doesn't totally reveal itself to me until I ask for his help with my high school physics homework. When I can't understand something he has so clearly explained, he prods me until I am in tears. After Granma's death, wishing to lessen his loneliness for a day, I arrive in Red Bud ready to bake for him. Never having been supervised in the kitchen before, I am unprepared to have each of my movements scrutinized—guaranteeing I'll make a poor job of this cherry pie and trying my patience in a way it has never been tested before. When I later seek sympathy from my mother, she says, "Now you have some idea what I've been through."

He soon marries a widow of long acquaintance, but they are not happy together. He remains able to stand on his head until one night he pulls the covers over his head and stops breathing.

Granpa's last gift to me is a copy of *The Rubaiyat of Omar Khayyam*— "Ah, take the cash and let the credit go!"—surprising not only because of its hedonistic message but also because I've never seen him with a book in his hand. I know that he wishes me a full life, including as much education as I want.

Dynamos of Hope

I'm famous among friends and neighbors for this crop—
    my only apron says it: "Lettuce Eat."
But even with long years of practice
    I am no model gardener.
My methods random—
    early records, notes abandoned.
I scatter way more seeds than recommended
    then mist and pray them in
    tendering respect for all the teams of life I cannot see.
Compost's worms officiate
    at this communion we create
    to consecrate this soil to give us food.
Isn't every seed a compact dynamo of hope?
    May you land well and sprout.
May it be so for my words:
    May you bloom above my sod of doubt.

CHAPTER 2

EARLY DAYS

After growing up in rural Red Bud, Illinois, my parents made a home in the St. Louis area. My childhood was spent in a modest rock-faced house in lower-middle class Rock Hill, a half hour west of downtown St. Louis.

MY BEGINNING

For virtually all of their three-year engagement, World War II put Dad on the other side of the globe. On one of his brief leaves, Orville Wetzel and Jean Finley marry in 1945.

Dad serves in Sydney, Australia, in the Navy as a shipping clerk while Mom works in clerical jobs at Laclede Steel in St. Louis. At his discharge in 1946, Dad arrives in St. Louis with no car, no contacts, no money, no place to live, and a new wife—and unable to feel proud of his war service, stuck as he was so far from the action.

Housing in those postwar years is tight. The newlyweds start out in a boardinghouse room with a hot plate, and the bathroom is down the hall. Dad finds an assembly-line job and studies at night for an engineering certificate, preparing him to work at the Missouri State Highway Department.

After three years of marriage, I am eagerly awaited, especially by Dad. In my baby book Mom writes that at six weeks I found my thumb, giving me immediate and continuing comfort.

When I'm twenty months old, my sister Linda dislodges me from the center of the universe. In my sleep I console myself by wrapping my hair toward my mouth with my thumb-hand. When this starts pulling out my hair, the solution is a boy's haircut. My first memory is in that Red Bud barbershop. Being called a "cute boy" really got my attention.

Linda and me post-barbershop

Then, twenty months after Linda comes Brian. We get along pretty well except when we're cooped up for too long. Once when Mom can't take our picking at each other for another minute, she says: "You kids are driving me crazy. I'm leavin'!" She looks back to see three little faces pressed against the window.

SISTERS

Lin and I have no trouble sharing a bed, even when she wakes me crying, "Janet, I wet the bed!" We just put a few wooden blocks under that spot and sleep around it. Once in the middle of the night she mistakes my hand under her pillow for a skeleton, and we have a laugh.

Linda's social, emotional, and physical intelligences exceed mine. When Dad's in his armchair reading the paper, she spies a way to fit into his lap without disturbing his paper. He nicknames her Kitten. Lin also slips easily into Mom's lap. I wish I could, but something restrains me. Walking to school, before turning the first corner, tenderhearted Linda looks back to wave at Mom, who's waiting to wave back. Turning around never occurs to me. Once Linda stops me in my tracks by saying, "You hurt my feelings." Even though I don't quite know what she means, I immediately sense that I've wronged her in a way that goes beyond jamming snow down her neck. I don't know how to put words to or signal what I'm feeling, and here she instinctively stands up for her feelings. She naturally makes friends at school and in our neighborhood.

When Granpa Finley presents us with our first tricycle, while I stand there looking at it, Linda climbs right on. Granpa offers a quarter to whoever climbs the thick rope he's affixed to a high branch. Linda and Brian pull themselves right up—I only manage a couple of yards. While I can't work out how to get my legs above my head, her cartwheels are perfection. For a number of weeks she's the fastest runner in our whole grade school.

ECONOMY AND RESTRICTIONS

After earning an engineering certificate after the war, Dad starts work at the Missouri State Highway Department as a surveyor. This job fits him well—not only does he excel at precise measurement and planning, he's also outdoors most of the time. But managerial roles are necessary to support three kids, so for three decades, he's unhappily stuck at a desk. Even so, economy is necessary and comes naturally to these two children of the Depression.

Mom and Dad take their responsibilities as parents more seriously than anything. Dad follows the Bible's exhortation: "Train up a child in the way he should go, and when he is grown, he will not depart from it." Choices are few; threats and punishments are unnecessary. It doesn't occur to me to push against restrictions, like only being allowed to bike two blocks from home except for the four blocks to school.

Only twice do I remember protesting anything. When Dad forbids my wearing my brand-new royal blue tights to church, I object (to no avail, of course). And on my first trip to the St. Louis Zoo at age seven, I beg for a snow cone. The day is mercilessly hot. Then I'm instructed to share it with Linda! When I pitch a fit, Mom says, "You're making me ashamed of you in front of my parents!"

Apparently by age eight I'm with the program. The night I'm in the hospital for a tonsillectomy, noticing I'm still awake, a nurse asks if I want something to help me sleep and slips something tiny and smooth up my butt—an odd new sensation—but my immediate worry is that this'll cost extra and Dad will be unhappy. Dad's thrift extends to instructing us to build our snowmen next to young trees for the extra moisture.

Mom's food budget is tight, but she's great at feeding us. Dad's hunting, usually with brothers in Illinois, puts deer and squirrel on the table; we also eat a lot of catfish. Because they are so infrequent, outings are very special—on a sweltering day sitting at Walgreens' air-conditioned soda fountain counter for a lemonade is a memorable treat.

NEIGHBORHOOD

Go-to summer activities are chasing the milkman, who kindly chops off pieces of ice from his giant block to hand out to sweaty kids; scrubbing the front porch with toothbrushes as a way to play with the hose and erase my crayoning; sitting in weedy grass scanning for four-leaf clovers, until giving up and making chains; and with the help of a ladder, climbing and reading in our black hickory, my first intimate relationship with a tree. All our barefoot summers, and I only get one bee sting.

There's only one girl my age in our ragtag couple of blocks; during her cousin's frequent visits, she ignores me. Still, I envy her easy access to treats and toys. Once when my parents are playing cards with friends from church, and we kids are in their basement, jealousy seizes me. One of their toys ends up in my pocket, even as I know that I'll have to return it at great inconvenience to my parents and shame to me.

A KINDLY NEIGHBOR

Our best neighbor is right next door. Lu Miller is often in her backyard, hanging wash or tending rhubarb or sitting on her stoop next to her silent husband, who's more than twice her size. Lu could overhear my singing to myself on the swing hanging from our doomed American elm and would have noticed my thumb-sucking and sympathized with my shy neediness.

One Christmas I receive a miniature baking set complete with tiny boxes of real cake mix. When my first one is iced, Mom suggests I take it to Lu, who often shares her cookies with us, though none of us like the cereal she puts in hers. Happy to find me at her door, Mrs. Miller welcomes me in to "sit a minute." She looks so comfortable in her kitchen chair, with her tiny feet in short white socks crossed at the ankles, her hands folded on her belly. Naturally I'm staring at my little cake, so she urges me to eat a piece. Coughing on the crumbs, I wonder why she wants me to eat the treat intended for her. Maybe she just likes my company.

FAILED PETS

My family hosts a series of failed pets. Our aged beagle, Tuffy, passes the end of his life sleeping in hay in the backyard. Next is Trusty, a beagle puppy meant for hunting who quickly belies his name and doesn't last long. Frosty, a white rat terrier, doesn't like any of us, barfs behind the couch, and runs away at every chance. The kitten Dinah climbs the screen door and screeches at night. We have a messy guppy phase, but no one likes to clean the tank. Finally we manage a happy arrangement with a parakeet. But one evening with the bird on my shoulder, I mindlessly walk out the door and he flies to freedom—and certain death. Devastated, I walk the neighborhood trying to call him down. For a while Dad raises rabbits, allowing us to play with the snow-white babies while making it clear that they are food, not pets.

BARBIE?

Pretend games baffle me—all those girls prancing around as ponies! And I can't figure out how to have fun with dolls. I'm jealous of the immense solitary happiness dolls bring my sister—until at age eleven Linda spends her little money on a Barbie, whereupon my thirteen-year-old self thinks less of her.

For a while paper dolls answer an urge. The Sears catalogue inspires my designs for new clothes for Natalie Wood, Debbie Reynolds, and Tuesday Weld. The mini-biographies I concoct for some of them repeatedly crack Brian up (one has "a boyfriend named George who has big hands and dirty knees").

Weeding

Dandelions, clover—I respect.
But spurge and pokeweed are competing with my baby lettuces
so I must gently fight to win in my raised bed.
My trowel turns over twenty at a time—
each green dot anchored by the finest threads
sure to sprout a legion more.

Tentative my touch—
roots of good entangle with the bad—
sometimes unclear
which to nurture, which to tear.

Where my little seedlings are packed tight
I extricate a few to fill in gaps.
When tendrils beg "don't move us yet"
I sprinkle extra seeds instead.

With aching back I'm humming "Wondrous Love"
and tracking songs of towhee, sparrow, yellow-rump
when a neighbor's leaf blower attacks
and blasts me into existential angst.

I've no defense—
stand paralyzed with dirty shoes and hands and pants—
must quit my task, go in and wash and wait.

Later I may lay me down in sunwarm grass
bare feet ahhhing thanks for this massage.
I arise without assist
and water in this coming food.

To bring forth any good—
though war goes seldom to the just—
we seek and take constructive rest
and battle what we must.

THE RELIEF OF RED BUD

Excitement builds on Saturday mornings as we close the distance to Red Bud, where treats await us. The Finleys' corner apartment is on the third floor of the only three-story building in town at the only stoplight. One block further on Main Street and turn the corner on Lincoln Street and one short block and there's the Wetzels' small house and big garden. Even when very young, we kids freely walk between these two very different and equally interesting abodes.

In between sits the dime store, where we're allowed a comic and sometimes even paper dolls. A few doors down is the creamery with unbeatable everything, especially root beer floats. But the very best is Gert's Dress Shop, where a few times a year Granma Finley buys Linda and me the most beautiful clothes that always fit perfectly. Gert is always very glad to see us.

MT. CALVARY LUTHERAN SCHOOL

"If you can't tie your shoes, you can't start kindergarten." Since I'd evidently been unable to learn this from anybody, I devise my own complicated way. Shame-tinged self-invention becomes a recurring theme.

Mom's photo from my first day of kindergarten shows me proudly erect, hands clenched to hide my bitten nails. A serious student is born— I'm gonna somehow prove how good I can be!

I'm the shortest in my class and sometimes wear hand-me-downs from girls in the grade above me (two grades are together in one schoolroom). The only other girl in my grade who's smart and obedient has beautiful hair, nails, smile, clothes, and shoes. While she's also very nice, I'm often conscious of her perfection.

During kindergarten I develop a crush on the principal's son, who is a year ahead of me. Even though he never looks at me, this unfortunate attraction continues throughout grade school. I never acknowledge this hopeless situation to anyone. Once I lose control and crayon MIKE on the back of a folding chair, not realizing how visible this would be when the chair is in use. A crisis occurs a few weeks before I start second grade when my mother asks the principal's family to dinner. We go barefoot during the summer, and since we haven't gone school shopping yet and we're not allowed to wear our Sunday shoes, I have none to wear and almost can't stand for Mike to see me.

As a child, I only have one occasional fantasy—my real parents, Dale Evans and Roy Rogers, rescue me from the clutches of doctors trying to give me shots. But no thought begins with "I wonder." Only two other pieces of evidence that I have any imagination survive. The night after seeing a TV show on the 1906 San Francisco earthquake, the shaking of my bed awakens me; I run down to tell Mom that our walls are going to fall and fires will start. Also, my left big toe reminds me of Tony Curtis after I see a movie starring him.

SINGLED OUT

Our kindergarten teacher labors with my class to prepare a Bible passage to recite at graduation. During the repetitive practice, the teacher says, "Sing out like Janet!" For a second I hold my head high. Then a queasiness sets in over being singled out.

In second grade I'm awarded a Bible for perfect Sunday School attendance. In fourth grade I win a competition for the fastest memorized repetition of the books of the Bible: "Genesisexodusleviticusnumbersdeuteronomy," et al., with one pause mid-Old Testament, and a longer one before launching into the New Testament. This prize is better—a Bible with a useful concordance and with *Janet Wetzel* embossed in fake gold on the fake leather cover. We are constantly served up Martin Luther's Small Catechism: "I, a poor miserable being, justly deserve Thy temporal and eternal punishment," and "Thou shalt not covet thy neighbor's wife, nor his manservant, nor his maidservant nor…" [etc.]. Many nonsensical paragraphs admonish that "This is most certainly true."

INSTRUCTIONS

We are actively discouraged from thinking for ourselves. The questions we are asked have only one correct answer. Every rule structures our awareness around obedience and punctuality. With the last name of Wetzel, I am always last in line—punctual and impatient. And whatever eye-to-hand creative urges survive hour upon hour of coloring within the lines, my first-grade teacher exterminates; she insists that each picture must begin with a horizon line.

Since we live so close to school, in nice weather we come home for lunch; Dad often drives home for lunch too from his office in nearby Kirkwood. One day I arrive home later than usual, so Dad asks me why. "Big black birds in a tree were screaming at me, and I couldn't walk near them." He replies, "Never be afraid of crows or any living creature—God gave man dominion." This instruction comes in handy with dogs too.

The only reading material at home besides cereal boxes are a few things from Mom's childhood and Bibles, read-to-shred comics, and the lifeless encyclopedias purchased from a traveling salesman. The only pages I study feature naked statues, but a big leaf covers the parts I'm interested in.

Little Rascals

skin's all wrinkled, hair is white
still in my veins they frolic—
playing hooky, fooling teacher
making cakes with a prize inside
praying to the genie in the lamp
washing my face in watermelon
hiding from the cops
c'mon, Petey! skipping and singing
it's Saturday, it's Saturday
hey nonny nonny and a ha-cha-cha!
    how can getting away with something not feel grand?
    asks the child, barefaced with hope
    and determined to keep playing.

ACHIEVEMENT ORIENTATION

Asked, "What do you want to be when you grow up?" I draw a blank. I wonder if it's questions like this that plant the terribly inaccurate impression that there's childhood and then "grown up." My only choices seem to be "mother," "teacher," or "nurse." I sometimes name "dentist's receptionist" as a possible future because the one in the office of my mean dentist is nice.

My achievement orientation first reveals itself at age nine: "Dear God, PLEASE let me be picked to play Gretel in the operetta; after all, I have the best voice!" (The only time I ever pray for a specific outcome in my whole life.) I don't remember much except a worry that Hansel won't remember his lines and then about a second's worth of applause at the end and the special dessert Mom makes. Surely I received some praise, but I don't remember ever being praised for anything. Kids in those days didn't expect much of it.

MUSICAL THRILL

Singing in the choir of my Lutheran grade school teaches me to read music; I love arrangements when I can sing harmony. With a polio-shriveled hand, our music director (who is also the principal and best teacher in the school) once plays us a recording of Handel's "Hallelujah Chorus," explaining that because this is the greatest sacred music ever written, we stand up for it. This is the most memorable hour of my grade school experience and the first musical thrill of my life.

In seventh grade, I get six months of piano lessons, then Linda gets six. Despite the limited abilities of my arthritic teacher and the awful recital pieces she selects for me, I love practicing and learn enough to be able to play any hymn and the easiest Bach, Chopin, and sheet music from favorite musicals (*South Pacific, Porgy and Bess*). Playing rivets my attention.

GIRL SCOUTS

Brownies followed by Girl Scouts is my only organized after-school activity. Wearing a green sash with mostly meaningless "merit" badges, we belt out the Girl Scouts' theme song embodying what girls in the 1950s were supposed to aspire to—sincerity, courtesy, loyalty. "She wears a G for generosity. She wears an I for interest, too. She wears an R for real sportsmanship. She wears and L for loyalty, for loyalty! She wears an S for her sincerity. She wears a C for courtesy. She wears an O-U-T for outdoor life, outdoor life. And that Girl Scout is Me!"

In case a husband's shirt needs one, we learn to sew on buttons. One girl rebels; she says she's never going to have a husband, much less one who loses buttons. I admire her clarity, even though the troop leader ridicules her reason. Once my troop puts on a play at another school; I am a cornhusk.

CONFIRMATION

God doesn't seem to have been invited to my confirmation into the Lutheran church at age thirteen. In any case, my galloping self-consciousness at being in front of the whole congregation and at finally getting to wear nylons, heels, and lipstick renders everything else meaningless.

There are only six in my eighth grade graduating class. My classmates select me to give the talk and to receive the award for Christian Excellence. That year my mom is the president of the Women's Guild, so she presents the award—a unique moment for us, somewhat marred by my having a black eye from practicing high jump on a contraption I jerry-rigged.

NEW RESPONSIBILITIES

In eighth grade when a neighbor asks me to babysit, I am over the moon—my first paid work. The only aspect I come to like, though, is sampling contents of their refrigerator and searching their books for any info about sex.

I'm also taking on new responsibilities at home. When Mom's in the hospital for her fibroid-necessitated hysterectomy, Dad expects me to put dinner on the table. Shortly thereafter she starts afternoon clerking at a department store candy counter, until the boss puts a move on her. Then she gets a much better job at the Rock Hill library (and within a decade is head librarian, as her own mother had been in Red Bud).

> "With growth into adulthood, responsibilities claimed me, so many heavy coats. I didn't choose them, I don't fault them, but it took time to reject them."—Mary Oliver

CHAPTER 3

GROWING PAINS

The shy thumb-sucking child becomes an even lonelier adolescent who devotes herself to excelling in public school. After meeting the love of my life in high school, ten years into our marriage, my drinking tears us apart.

BODY SHAME

Even before my body starts to change, I'm already ashamed of it. In un-air-conditioned Missouri summers, Lin and I don't wear tops in our yard. At age six or seven, I'm with a neighbor girl two years older who points at my chest, saying, "Aren't you ashamed!" In a flash I'm naked—Eve cast out of the garden, forever. And the first naked woman I see (in a bath house), pendulous bulges quivering, terrifies me—I run for cover.

In eighth grade a Girl Scout-distributed booklet on menstruation compounds my shame and confusion. In shock, I read it over and over. What is the matter with me that all these years I've been clueless about this? As all my female classmates achieve this supposedly blessed state, now there's something else for me to feel defective about.

POWERLESS

I develop later than my peers. My same-age cousin and her always preferred buddy tease me for my naivete. I HATE my dingy undershirts and spend hours staring at the bra pages in the Sears catalogue.

When my breasts finally start to emerge (I try not to sleep face-down in case this helps), I'm inexplicably unable to talk to Mom about a bra or to undress in front of Lin. What for years I've longed to have, I'm now massively self-conscious of.

Pursuing every sly opportunity to corner me and grope my breasts, my older male cousin becomes the bane of my existence (our families visit often during these years and camp together). I'm also terrified of my orthodontist, who rubs my breasts right before sadistically tightening my braces. I am powerless.

My hands break out in a weeping, relentlessly itching rash. The school nurse feels sorry for me—there's apparently no remedy.

FIRST DRIVING LESSON

My first driving lesson is also my first lesson in the importance of knowing when to stay out of Dad's way at night. I'm just fourteen in my baby doll pj's when, drunk, he gets it in his head to teach me to drive. I've never been behind any wheel before, apart from navigating a bike, which he should remember did not come naturally to me. Terrified and lacking any sense of what I'm supposed to be doing, I manage two blocks before the car ends up on an incline in someone's front lawn, right as a group of boys I know from church are walking by. Dad pushes me to the floor, scoots into the driver's seat, and when the boys quizzically approach, makes up some ridiculous excuse.

LEARNING TO KISS

The summer after tenth grade, finally released from braces and the infection on my hands, I'm dying to attract a boy's attention. But shy and friendless, I have few options. M, a girl in my class, sporadically finds me useful, like when she needs a back-up dancer for her failed talent show number to the tune of "Come have a fling, come to the Mardi Gras!"

The payoff of knowing M is an invitation to double date, although all we do is park. She's eager to break into the thespian club, and our dates, who are one year older than us, are members. As she giggles in the front seat, in the back seat I am indeed fortunate to be inaugurated into necking by a nice quiet guy with a firmly closed mouth and strong arms attached to non-groping hands. This encounter spurts some unprecedented neurochemical into my bloodstream that eliminates my appetite for a few days—how welcome and fascinating!

Later that same summer of 1965, Granpa Finley takes me and my same-age cousin H on a Greyhound bus trip from St. Louis to Mexico. We are joining a group of retired teachers. He is the only male, and H and I are the only females under sixty. San Antonio is the first stop. As our group walks along a sidewalk near the Alamo, H and I are easy targets for GIs on the make. Granpa is delighting in the attentions of all those women, and H is delighting in the attentions of a GI, one of whom steers us into a frigid theater showing *Goldfinger,* where a khaki-clad adolescent proceeds to slobber all over my face.

Opportunistic cornering of young women is even more rampant in Mexico. On public buses, it's almost impossible to escape the hands. Both of our charming local tour guides go after my cousin. On our first evening at the Acapulco beach hotel, while swimming in the pool H and I meet an actually nice group of boys our age from Peru who speak enough English. Pato takes a special interest in me and isn't put off by my glasses. The next day finds us in my hotel room. As he encourages me toward the bed, I say, "No, I'm Lutheran." Even though I can't explain why that's relevant, he doesn't push me. But later after rolling around on the beach, I find bewildering white stains on my skirt. We actually write to each other a few times. Pato calls me "mi reina" (my queen). But after I point out that Shakespeare wrote the poem that he claims to have authored, that's the end of that.

On our last night in Mexico, cornered in the restaurant by a rougher character, I'm lucky to emerge with only whisker burns all over my face and neck. This visible evidence finally awakens Granpa to what's been going on all week. He blames me.

JUNIOR HIGH SCHOOL

I achieve mental liftoff in ninth grade via the refreshing logic of algebra and geometry and the leap-off-the-page human beings in Dickens. *David Copperfield* is my first chapter book not written for girls. I seem to be the only one besides the teacher who likes it; the school newspaper says, "We hate it like the Dickens!" Prior to this, my only books of note are *Anne of Green Gables* (the first book to reduce loneliness), *Nancy Drew*s, and orange-covered biographies of the wives of early presidents.

Most of the other students in my junior high class have been together for two years. Until the last week of ninth grade, I feel like an outsider. Then, apparently because I am studious and organized, I'm elected president of our little Tri-Hi-Y group. The group's main function is to host quarterly dances at the YMCA. But no one ever asks me to dance, raising further doubts as to my social acceptability and dating prospects. I am so sick of Johnny Mathis' number, "Chances Are," repetitively humiliating me while everybody else slow dances.

On the two opportunities when I invite a boy to something, I am turned down. I fling myself upon my bed and find a tad of comfort in Psalm 43: "Why art thou cast down, O my soul? And why art thou disquieted within me? Hope in God."

Loneliness

Have you got used to loneliness?
What's lost when you hole up inside?
Don't longings beg to be expressed—
Not hollowed out in loneliness?
What is unfreezing in your chest?
What wants to be confided?
Don't get used to loneliness.
Find someone to sit beside.

HIGH SCHOOL

Webster Groves High School is a building four times larger than any I've ever entered and also under construction. My homeroom is about as far away as it can be from my first period class; finding my way becomes a source of nightmares.

Linda has no problem adapting to public school. Naturally, with her spirit and ability to cartwheel and do the splits, she becomes a cheerleader. She's elected to student government too, and as a sophomore, dates guys in my class before I do!

The only specific advice my engineer dad ever gives me is "Take as much math and science as you can." Going against my counselor's advice, I take physics, which is much harder for me than any other course, unrelated to being the only girl in the class.

To help me work off the stress, my brother Brian plays Ping-Pong and softball catch with me.

FIRST REAL DATE

A quiet guy, a year older, from my church group asks me to play mini-golf. Since I've never even been asked to dance, this represents such progress! Lighting a cigarette, D is delighted when "I Can't Get No Satisfaction" comes on his car radio. Not allowed to listen to rock at home and having as yet no experience with double negatives, I don't understand the lyrics, but the music and his love of the song thrill me. Necking in his front seat is fun without ever being too hot to handle, and he enjoys my company way more than anyone else seems to. After the couple I'm babysitting for arrive home early and embarrass us on the couch, I don't hear from D again.

During junior year, when a boy in my class of five hundred finally asks me out, I tolerate his inability to talk to me; he doesn't even touch me.

EPIPHANY

At the end of that summer I am reading Maugham's *Of Human Bondage*. At a small lake resort, my family is enjoying what we know will be our last summer vacation together. Walking along the lake, as the first evening star appears I have the first epiphany of my life: Why am I staying in bondage to this boring boy? I can get contact lenses! And I can lose weight (with the help of a few amphetamines offered by a woman I babysit for)! I glimpse another way of being.

In a few months I am pretty and flirt-worthy.

MY FIRST DRINK AND MY FIRST DATE WITH BILL

In senior year as literary editor of the yearbook, I am thrown together with Bill because he is the art editor. He's also in my English class. I've been longing for him to ask me out. When our friend C, the head editor, invites us to a meeting in her basement, she offers us a few sips of her grandfather's bourbon. I am never the same. When the first molecules of high-proof alcohol enter my bloodstream, they fit perfectly into my brain's receptors, proclaiming, "This is the best possible thing that could be happening!!!" The whole world sparkles in technicolor—for about ten minutes (I metabolize it like mad). We laugh ourselves silly.

As Bill drives me home, he asks me for a date. I'm flying. Then later I think: Maybe I could ask him to procure some alcohol for our date. But this feels very awkward. Shame and confusion pollute my joy and excitement.

On Valentine's Day, from the nice guy I dated in the fall I receive a Debussy album and my first stationery, and from a rich but homely and narcissistic guy, a silver bracelet with my name engraved, which I give right back. At the end of classes that Valentine's Day, Bill leads me to his locker, from which he presents me with a dozen red roses. Not only is he clever and cute (except for the acne and glasses), he's also the first person who wants to get to know me, my first friend. We are in love. At the prom, dancing as close together as we can get to the Temptations' "My Girl," we are in heaven.

Petting

reclining on sweet hay—
    I sigh transported
    as on my chest you purr
    and knead me, careful of your tiny knives
    and touch your sweet wet nose to mine
do you know my scent
    or will you soon forget—
    maybe anybody's hands would do
    but carpe diem
    we have fun, we two.

A few weeks after graduation, under the blessedly privacy-giving willow trees in St. Louis' Forest Park, he asks me to marry him. When I wake my mother, she half-weeps, "You're too young!" So secure are we in our new-found happiness that we're oblivious to the gamble this decision represents.

After seeing each other every day since we started dating six months earlier, when Bill goes on vacation with his family, I'm woebegone, reduced to frequent checking of the mailbox. Sometimes I play the piano for consolation. One of those days, fifteen-year-old Lin (in payback for past wrongs or maybe just sick of my pining around) leaps out to scare me. I burst into tears. Standing nearby, Dad reprimands her, "That's mean. She's missing Bill." (This is the only spontaneous tenderness on his part I ever witness.)

SUMMER JOBS

The spring I turn sixteen I get an odd kind of break. While babysitting for the Rich family, a drunken uncle shows up and starts chasing me around the house. His hands are only inches away when Mr. and Mrs. Rich arrive. Driving me home, Mr. Rich assures me that if I need a summer job, I can come by his office (figuring that I will be telling my father what's happened and not wanting to lose my services). This sounds excellent to Dad—summer jobs are hard to land.

Mr. Rich's stockbrokerage firm employs me for the next three summers—endless over-air-conditioned days alphabetizing little slips of paper and typing with FIVE pieces of CARBON paper (one mistake means starting over).

The tight cubicle that houses the securities is called "the cage." The brokers bring their paperwork to the counter along with clients they are fawning over. They freely ogle us females behind the counter. The three heavily teased-out and made-up women with whom I share these close quarters continuously chitchat about dating and drinking escapades. One once spends half a morning in the bathroom applying makeup over a black eye.

My last summer job is even more useless—GS-5 clerk-typist for the Army Air Force. No one seems to have any work to do. My boss starts drinking at noon and rarely reappears. The next most senior guy is a loudmouth whose job is color coordinating the building's fire escape plans! One hunched old woman always dressed in black knits all day in an unlit corner. Not allowed to read, I pass the time discovering how hard it is to make up crossword puzzles.

COLLEGE

My senior-year English teacher asks where I'll be attending college.

"Drury College," I reply.

"You can do much better than that. Apply to Kalamazoo College, Grinnell, and Denison. You'll be accepted."

This is my first indication that I can shoot higher than seems to be the plan.

Drury's in Missouri, and I've won a scholarship there. Dad is in the middle of purchasing a long-desired rural property, plus Linda and Brian will also be needing help with college. He fills out the three applications for financial aid—to no avail. My teacher urges me to select Kalamazoo College in Michigan, and Dad agrees to pay the tuition.

Academically Kalamazoo is an excellent fit. Every course is well-taught and challenges me. In addition to art history, English composition, and Shakespeare, I take physics, calculus, philosophy, and a seminar on the philosophy of science. I have way more fun spending my $100 bookstore credit "scholarship" than any other $100 in my life.

Complementing these riches, two girls on my hall become my first girlfriends. My roommate Deb and I spend many happy hours talking in the dark; she is very private, and fortunately for me, deep and patient, especially with my repetitive playing of my Temptations album. Ann, also shy, becomes our pal. (Another plus: Ann's roomie teaches me to knit.)

My first month, in a very long letter Granpa Finley spells out the dangers of drugs (he's been reading *Time* magazine). Since I want to be experimenting along these lines almost more than anything else ("Sergeant Pepper" is on everywhere), I barely finish reading his lecture. If anybody had advised me against taking up smoking in college, likewise I wouldn't have heeded it. Nothing is easier for me than getting hooked on cigarettes.

I'm surprised, though, by how dreadfully homesick I am. That fades, but with a seventeen-hour bus ride between us, I can't bear three more years away from Bill. We write each other every day. He artistically decorates envelopes with hearts and cartoon characters expressing adoration. Soon my wall is plastered with these, and other girls stop by to wonder at the ever-widening display. He also sends roses on just the right occasions.

When he can finally visit, desperate to be alone together, I garner the cooperation of girls in my hall so I can sneak him into my room for a few hours. The next day, the loudspeaker in the cafeteria is blaring "Janet Wetzel, report to the dean's office." Snitched on by one of the jealous girls, I am sentenced to a term of proctoring the dorm lounge, separating boys and girls and kicking boys out at closing time. It's all so ridiculous—within a few years, boys and girls will be sharing dorms!

When Bill Greyhounds up to give me my engagement ring on my nineteenth birthday, Ann and Deb fete us (Ann takes the photo on the back cover). Intent on sleeping with Bill, I talk a girl in my hall into lending me her duvet; Bill finds a damp field for us to bed down in. We awaken to a red sun. As Bill recites "Red sun at night, sailors' delight; red sun at dawning, sailors' take warning!" we run to the car, already drenched. I don't know what I did about the soaked duvet.

Hush

Until I'm clearing parents' walk of gently falling snow
    beneath an arch of Christmas lights
    I didn't know
    how much I'd longed for just this winter combo.

My whole being smiles—
    with cat upon my lap before a fire
    we purr
    of joys unspeakable.

Sunrise scatters diamonds on the fields.
    Brush piles entertain like puzzles—
    mazes of tracks of deer and squirrels and rabbits
    swish of mice, clawed alphabet of birds.

This silent life pulls me to stay
    but I am bound for company
    and far away from winter woods
    where hush does not convey.

UNIVERSITY OF MISSOURI

Transferring to the University of Missouri for sophomore year saves money; we want to get married without having to borrow from our folks. At Kalamazoo, on Friday and Saturday nights I wiped down never-ending dining room tables with a smelly gray rag. During the next three years, after giving up housecleaning jobs in disgust, I'm stuck in a cashier's stall in Mizzou's Student Commons on Saturday and Sunday nights, where the jukebox's "Hey Jude" and "Born to be Wild" repeatedly assault me.

Since Bill doesn't own a car and dorm lounge rules are just as restrictive as at Kalamazoo, being together at college is not nearly as much fun as I'd imagined. The quality of dorm life is also a comedown. The main focus of my dorm mates (lots of sorority rejects) is boys, and by extension, football and beer. Once a beery girl walks into my room, where I'm reading in bed, as usual; she laughs as she takes off my glasses and smears them with her saliva. In the cafeteria I'm the only girl who reads. Corresponding with Ann and Deb helps keep me going.

A few of my required courses are a waste. When I show up for the English Composition final, the instructor says, "What are you doing here? You could teach this!" (Then why didn't you spare me a semester of your flirting with the sorority cuties?) For the Psychology 101 lectures shown on a small black-and-white TV, the ancient professor is visibly dying of cancer.

But my courses in the Honors College are a semi-guided heaven of exploring great minds of the past. I do not notice that all the artists, philosophers, and most of the authors I've read in high school and college are male.

"Happiness surprises in both its advent and its causes: it releases information."—Louise Glück

LIBERAL ARTS EDUCATION

My strong liberal arts education, acquired inside and outside the classroom, never stops growing in value. In college, Bill introduces me to jazz and blues via his ever-growing collection of LPs. Along with the Beatles and Frank Zappa, jazz becomes a shared pleasure, with both of us favoring tenor sax—almost as subtly and sexily expressive as the human voice. Bill takes me to the St. Louis Art Museum, initiating a lifetime of enjoyment of museums together. Mizzou's four-semester Honors Humanities sequence, taught by the university's best professors in art history, architecture, philosophy, and literature, opens civilization's treasures to us. My first visits to the Metropolitan Art Museum and MOMA knock my socks off. We also take advantage of free drama and musical productions at college.

ENGLISH AND EDUCATION MAJOR

Emily Dickinson ("Debauchee of Dew"), Walt Whitman ("Out of the cradle endlessly rocking"), and Thoreau's odes to the out-of-doors enthrall me, initiating a lifelong craving for literature. Devoting entire days to classics like James Baldwin's *Go Tell It on the Mountain* and Herman Melville's *Moby-Dick* multiplies their impact. I thrive on the assignments to research critical interpretations and then synthesize them into my own assessment—hours spent sorting through heavy drawers of little cards and scribbling down call numbers, then wandering in the stacks until finally pulling a book.

In love with Shakespeare, Blake, Keats, et al., I major in English. Even with all my As, not one of the all-male English faculty asks if I'm considering graduate school. In 1970 we still wore "gender blinders." We didn't notice women's absence from the educated professions or how, in Disney movies, Wendy is left at home darning Peter Pan's socks.

Knowing I'll need to get a job upon graduation and unable to come up with an alternative, I take all the courses necessary for secondary teaching certification. The education courses are poorly taught and seem contentless; I endeavor not to dwell on the pitiful irony of this.

However, student-teaching fully engages me. To the amazement of my supervisor, tenth graders who've been passed along as dumb or unmotivated enthusiastically respond to the writing prompts I supply from comics, TV shows, and Dylan and Stones lyrics. Perpetually feeling like one, I identify with outcasts and underdogs. I also develop and teach an elective on the Bible as Literature.

Can You Sonnet Spring?

The writing of this sonnet is beyond me
despite my teacher's urging me so strongly.
The problem is that words can't give a hint,
can't summon one sweet soupçon of the scent
of the glad exuberance of spring:
songs, hues, and tender tips beyond describing,
brown thrasher's couplets, intricate and rhyming,
peepers' sleighbells' near and distant chiming,
bloodroot's cupping petals, drenched in white—
we're thrilling to the lengthening of light—
tiny Dutchman's-breeches, yellow cuffed.
No praise of her particulars enough!
Locked in a scanning jail of fourteen lines
spring overflows all metrical confines.

FIRST PURCHASE

That Missouri's legal drinking age is 21 enables me to make better use of college. On the long-awaited day in 1970 when I can finally purchase something, I nervously enter the liquor store, never having been in one before. I choose a cheap white wine that I have no way of chilling. I drink it warm and sour, pretending I am celebrating.

WEDDING

Bill and I wait until right before senior year, when we've saved enough money to get started on our own. How we long to get married and how ready I am to leave home. Heavier than ever, Dad's drinking ruins my last summer. I obsess that he will show up at our ceremony drunk. But I'm the one who's sneaking sips of vodka in my closet.

I plan a simple wedding. Our yearbook friend sews my dress, covering the top of an oatmeal container with satin, from which descends the lace of my veil. The service Bill and I design and the church basement reception go off without a hitch. Our families are very happy for us, and we're blessed to have Bill's Granma Russell and my Granma Wetzel and Granpa Finley there.

Granpa and I

Bill, Me, Mom, Dad

I'd started on the birth control pill that Mom's ancient gynecologist prescribed. Within a month, I regained the ten pounds I'd dieted the year to lose. And my cramps triple. During our first months, when I'm weeping in bed, Bill reads me *Mad* magazine to try to make me laugh. The brand of pills I started on is shortly taken off the market for killing rats. The next brand I try works well for years.

the multiplicities of one

the mountain peaks of fun
the crucible of family
the scouring pad of envy
the rocking chair of worry
the handcuffs of old jealousy
the consolations of hot tea
the heaven of a baby's scent
the warm fires of accomplishment
the virus of resentment
the sacrament of peaches
the therapy of beaches
the hula hoop of laughter
the vacuum of day after
the stretching rack of hindsight
the empty room of being right
the quicksand of rejection
the soft sun of affection
the open door of kinship
the tendrils of a friendship.

WE'RE PUT HERE TO LOVE

CHAPTER 4

BOTTOMING OUT AND LEARNING TO LIVE SOBER

"A great deal of chaos in the world occurs because people don't appreciate themselves. Having never developed sympathy or gentleness toward themselves, they do not experience harmony or peace, and therefore what they project to others is also inharmonious and confused."—Chögyam Trungpa

MOVING EAST

Bill and I are more than ready to leave Confederate flag-loving Columbia, Missouri. His art teachers have encouraged him to enroll at the Rhode Island School of Design (RISD). So during spring break of our senior year, we drive East for the first time. I've set up interviews at six high schools. No job offer is forthcoming. Figuring I'm doomed to a secretarial job and that dictation might be required, I try to teach myself shorthand. No can do.

Shortly after graduation, we pack our few belongings and head to Rhode Island. From a cheap motel in Woonsocket, we hunt for an apartment in Providence. Everything feels very strange and hard. Bill is so nervous he has the dry heaves in the morning. The two-roomer we land on Meeting Street is only a few blocks from the Brown and RISD campuses. But I almost weep to discover how expensive basic housekeeping items are.

The first year or two of marriage, for those without the sobering benefit of living together a while first, delivers gut-punching disappointments. Young women of my generation didn't realize how fairy tales like Cinderella convinced our subconscious that once we'd hooked Prince Charming, we were on easy street. I don't know how to respond when Bill demonstrates the proper way to button a shirt out of the dryer. In my family, we threw clothes on hangers. As his method seems like make-work, a vague resentment takes root and begins to silently flourish. Another kind of hiding begins when, finding a cigarette butt in the toilet, Bill explodes, asking if I wanted to die of lung cancer (as he feared his dad would from smoking, which he does thirteen years later). I am going to have to be more careful not to leave a trace.

First Anniversary

what could we have done
do now to keep
the peace between us
from shattering into these little pieces?

BROWN UNIVERSITY

I take the first job I am offered—temporary secretary at Brown University. My first assignment is transcribing the lab notes dictated by a Swiss physiologist. The pitiful bleating of the sheep he is experimenting on is easier to make out than his heavily accented English. When I fail at this, I'm transferred to Economics. Soon Brown's Office of the President hires me. On one of his frequent visits to the President, the new medical school's development officer encourages me to step into their opening for student affairs assistant.

Finally I can contribute something besides a perfectly typed page. But it's baptism by fire: With no prior exposure to medical education and no help, I find I am responsible for medical student admissions, financial aid, student affairs, social events, and staffing the curriculum committee. I only overlap with the person I'm replacing for one day. Her first instruction is to refill the stapler. Since I can't figure out how, I muddle around until I staple my finger. Now I'm bleeding all over her desk. What a start.

MEDICAL SCHOOL

The force behind Brown's fledgling medical school is Pierre Galletti, MD, PhD (he is also the sheep investigator). Dr. Galletti only meets with me a few minutes a week, leaving me with more questions than answers. I seek the counsel of officials at the university level. No one in admissions or financial aid has any experience with a twelve-month calendar or a professional school. Brown's associate admissions director is more interested in showing off his life-size *Playboy* centerfold affixed to his closet door than in assisting me.

So it's the students who teach me what they need. Many are near my age. Bill and I enjoy camping and hiking with a few of them. I become a dyed-in-the-wool student advocate.

After a year of working together, Dr. Galletti asks me where I see myself in five years. No one has ever asked me anything like this, so I have no response. He suggests I work toward a master's degree in Sociology while I continue to work full-time. Since I cannot afford tuition, he initiates a special arrangement with the dean's office. Augmenting my daily work with premed and medical students in this experimental program (seven years from college freshman to medical degree), I study their short- and long-term perspectives about medicine. To our disappointment, we find that enrollment in the longitudinal program neither reduces the level of anxiety the premeds experience nor encourages them to take more non-premed—i.e., liberal arts—courses.

VALUES DISSOLVING

Before long, unhappy with his options there, Bill drops out of RISD. During the months it takes him to find an entry-level graphic design job, I am very jealous of his freedom.

At this point I'm drinking every day. I'm constantly preoccupied by the need to keep Bill from noticing and by the challenge of procurement, as there's no package store within walking distance. I had decided to forgo driving after witnessing two drivers on Angell St. intentionally crashing into each other. I manage with cheap wine and cannabis (purchased from my Brown mail dude).

Except for a couple of medical students, the only friends we make are into drugs. Bill and I sample just about everything. We prize LSD's visual- and music-enhancing capabilities, but I easily weird out. Our closest friend recommends that we allow him to inject an evening's worth of pharmaceutical cocaine. I sing the body electric! Even though I know that this was a "one shot" deal, for a few days it's all I can think about, obsessively staring at and touching where the drug entered my arm.

During the three years when I'm working full-time and studying for my master's in Sociology, there's less time to party, but all this imbibing is dissolving my values and what little common sense I have.

When two men in positions of authority pursue me, I am entirely vulnerable—and cute and mini-skirted. At one point I seek help from Brown's health center director and from a clinical psychologist, but their questions fall wide of the mark of my difficulties. Anyway, I was incapable of admitting the whole truth about my drinking to anyone. Often when I wake up, I'm nothing but a regret-filled headache.

GEOGRAPHIC CURE?

One particularly hungover morning, I take an alcoholism test in a magazine; my stomach turns over at this evidence. Also, a friend had recently told me that the admissions committee's chairman had noticed alcohol on my breath during our meetings. I need a way out. It's time anyway. The first dean of the newly accredited medical school is taking over some of my roles. And I've just completed my master's. After the ceremony, the only way I know to celebrate is to treat myself to an entire bottle of wine.

Bill and I never feel at home in New England and mafia-run Providence anyway. I formulate the notion of spending the next nine months touring Europe, figuring that our tight budget and my inability to speak the languages will prevent me from drinking. (I learn later that this kind of pointless ploy is known as seeking a "geographic cure.")

We pack up our lives. Frommer's *Europe on $10 a Day* becomes our Bible. Of course, we have cheap wine at dinner, and I sneak ways to drink. Twice wrestling with corkscrews, I jab myself and require stitches.

We take glorious advantage of opera and art museums in Britain, Spain, Germany, Italy, and France. But I'm often lonely and wishing for the solitude in which to drink. We go weeks without hearing English.

MOVE TO THE WASHINGTON, DC, AREA

Returning from our cultural trek, once again with no job, contacts, or furniture, we select the DC area because of the possibility of government work and because it's not Missouri or New England or too far south. Stuck in a dismal motel while we look for an apartment, I am besieged by worry and find little to do but eat and study maps of Arlington's crazy streets. Within a week we find a two-roomer in Rosslyn, with an easy bus ride into DC.

I'm relieved that the first job to come through for me is at the Association of American Medical Colleges (AAMC). I'm hired into a soft money, tiny-cubicle, data-checking job. After all those recent weeks touring Venice, Florence, Paris (without standing in a single line, in 1977), I am so bored that a mouse represents welcome company. So I continue to interview.

REUNITED WITH MEDICAL STUDENTS

Then, thanks to the promotions of two staff members, within a year the best possible position opens up. Each medical school annually elects one enthusiastic student to represent it to AAMC. I function as these smart young adults' ally and link to the whole hierarchy of white-haired men above them. Heart pounding during governance meetings, I'm often serving as these underdogs' sole advocate. At one point, the AAMC president backs me against my office wall with his finger inches from my chest and declaims, "Your job is to keep these students out of my hair, and you're not doing it!" Clearly, he and I differ in our interpretations of my role.

I'm continually learning from and discovering the needs of medical students all over the country. I author regular reports educating them on such noncurricular topics as taking part in the health legislation process, understanding economic changes affecting medical practice, and partnering effectively with nurses. During away-from-home spring and annual meetings, I party with them. A few times things get out of hand.

FRANTIC

Fast-forward downhill: One night I get so stoned at a friend's apartment that I pass out and don't come home. Bill spends a frantic night looking for me. While he drives us home, a wolf is eating my heart out. I spend the morning with a six-pack in a nearby park. I could hardly have more contempt for myself, and yet I'm still far from bottoming out.

During this period I have a terrifying dream that I'm unable to examine because it signals such a damning degree of self-involvement: I look into a mirror and my head has become a monstrous Miss Piggy.

Bill and I are barely communicating. I can't answer any of his accusatory questions about my behavior. And he's finding everything associated with our purchase of and move into our first house extremely stressful.

LEAVING HOME

T, a physician twice my age who works on my floor, courts me. Starved for that kind of attention and living in a fairyland enabled by cannabis, I move in with him. With Bill trying to reason with me, I cram belongings into two trash bags and turn my back on the house I'd waited my whole life for, but am blindly giving up after only six months.

A month later, I don't know who I am. I spend hours staring at patterns in T's Persian rugs while he reproaches me for deficits over which I am powerless. He finally says, "You need to see a psychiatrist." I can't sleep. In desperation, digging through my trash bags of belongings, I locate the list of psychiatrists that my internist gave me a year earlier when he diagnosed me as alcoholic. As his use of this label sent me reeling, I can hardly believe that I kept this list. Something in me wants to live.

have you ever been missing?

I remember when
I was missing to myself
a cipher with a headache
fast-beating hollow heart
aquiver in a rabbit hole
until out fell the bottom
I landed on my knees
a hand reached down.

HELP

I call the first name on the list of psychiatrists. When I meet Joan a few days later, she advises me to move out ASAP, and I do. The only friend I have at this point welcomes me into her apartment; luckily for me, she's been wanting to move in with her boyfriend. T gives me the perfect excuse to leave him—he accuses me of cheating on him!

After I move out, he calls me drunk, pleading for my return, threatening suicide. I get him to promise to be out of his apartment when I come to get my plastic bags of belongings. A dozen red roses sit beside a note begging me to stay. With a shout of freedom driving over Key Bridge, I pitch the roses out the window.

BYOL

The psychiatrist also recommends Alcoholics Anonymous. The local AA phone number is easy to find and is answered on the first ring: "So the meeting nearest your office is BYOL—it meets every day at noon."

"What kind of sick joke is that?"

"The L stands for Lunch, not Liquor."

BYOL meets in a basement room of St. Matthews, Washington, DC's most beautiful cathedral. A well-dressed gentleman opens the door for me. I hear faint organ music. At my first meeting, someone talks about feeling guilty for wanting to drink, which is how I've felt since age seventeen but could never admit. I am home.

But at this point my life is way too complicated for me to actually stop drinking. The little control and judgment I used to be able to summon abandon me. I land in such humiliating situations—including the only unprotected sex of my life, followed by a month of breast-swollen terror—that I'm finally reduced to what AA calls "pitiful and incomprehensible demoralization."

> "No part of our hard-wiring or messy selves is to be disparaged. Where we stand, in all our mistakes and imperfection, is holy ground, where God chooses to be intimate with us."
> —Father Gregory Boyle

SUMMARY OF TESTING PSYCHOLOGIST'S REPORT

Age 31, Mrs. Janet Bickel was referred for psychiatric care due to alcohol abuse. She has strong dependency needs, which she denies. She tends to form attachments in search of total, uncritical acceptance. Her sense of autonomy is poorly developed. There is much unresolved anger directed toward parental figures and parental standards. She is also experiencing conflict between her high achievement orientation and her femininity. She has sufficient ego strength for intensive psychotherapy. Care must be taken to maintain optimal anxiety as her endurance is low.

"The world will ask you who you are, and if you don't know, the world will tell you."—Carl Jung

MOVING BACK

At the same time, Bill and I have begun dating and tentatively discussing my moving back. I am paralyzed by my instability and indecision. Concluding that I'd irredeemably fucked up my life, I return to BYOL on my knees. Someone offers to take me to a second meeting, and after listening to my tortured ramblings about whether I'm an alcoholic, he simplifies it for me: "If alcohol has more power over you than you want it to have, then you're probably an alcoholic and AA can help you." Bingo. That night, what feels exactly like God's fingertips haul a ton of bricks off my shoulders. I begin regular attendance.

So the first step, "We admitted we were powerless over alcohol—that our lives had become unmanageable," and the second step, "Came to believe that a Power greater than ourselves could restore us to sanity," occur simultaneously for me. I could not accept how intolerable my life had become until I could see a way out of it. Until I glimpsed how AA could help me, I couldn't accept my powerlessness—what would be the point?[1]

---

1 Although Alcoholics Anonymous was founded on the principle of anonymity, here I cannot remain anonymous. Since AA's founding, the disease's stigma has gradually declined in severity, largely because of AA, so perhaps my infringement is insignificant.

if tears arrive

If tears arrive behind your eyes
when you are folding underwear
what's heaving in those unsighed sighs?
What's hiding in your saddest lies?
Where have you stored your uncried cries?
Your heart must be too raw to bare
if tears arrive behind your eyes
when you are folding underwear.

GETTING SOBER

Naturally, after ten years of almost daily drinking, alcohol's voice can still trump AA's. At the first party I unwisely venture into, I'm so jealous of the twinkles in the eyes of those with a drink in hand that I readily succumb.

Also, I'm still imbibing small amounts of cannabis, enabling hours lost in "Janet is special" land, staring at ice cube prisms and pretending that I'm writing the Great American Novel (no matter that later I couldn't read my scribbles). At the end of my last little stash, I can't concentrate for a few days. But I'm ready to quit—I'm so motivated to locate some solid ground within myself.

Nervous as hell about getting through my first AAMC annual meeting sober (five days of nonstop responsibilities for multiple sessions, always with a shitload of hitches and drinking opportunities), I collect advice from BYOL ("keep candy and plenty of phone numbers handy"). On my way up to the Washington Hilton, I buy a bag of M&Ms—and a pint of vodka. The dominant voice in my brain is wheedling me: "Who are you kidding—you can't get through this without a little help!" When I return to my AA group, a friend asks me how it went. I mention the vodka, and when she says, "Oh, you had a slip," I want to slap her. The truth shall set you free, but first it'll piss you off!

Later that week a constituent stores a box of half-empty liquor bottles in my office. Although I need to be in my office, I know that if I stay, the booze will win because it would be *so* easy to sneak some from each bottle. I ask a colleague to store the booze. The meaning of "surrender to win" becomes clear. Finally I can walk away from the fight.

"Only when I yearn, do I learn / and what helps me grow is holy."
—Poet Gregory Orr, from "Lines Standing in for Religious Conviction."

JOAN

I continue to see Joan, the psychiatrist. My appointments are early in the morning. Sometimes she seems to fall asleep mid-session. I put myself through the mill wondering if I am that boring or if she's pretending to nod off as a test to see how I'll respond (I learn later that she has a substance abuse problem).

I stand up to her, however, in my decision to move back in with Bill. She believes that this move will interfere with the work of depending on myself. She's right, but Bill and I are ready to start rebuilding our marriage.

A Tribute to Joan

On the day when I first closed your door
I could not hear my wheelchair's whir.
Now I can tell my footstep from a crutch-tap nine times of ten.
You keep me focused on my limps and on the hard work that remains—
I broach this new path cautiously and sure of growing pains.

RETURNING TO OUR MARRIAGE

Staying sober doesn't automatically improve relationships. This comes as a very unwelcome surprise. Bill and I are indeed fortunate that Joan hooks us up with Carmen, who she calls the Cadillac of marriage counselors. (As an LSW in the 1980s, she only charges $35/hour!) Carmen opens by advising that we avoid "that four-letter word, Love—what we are talking about are Trust and Respect." Later she tells me that her first impression of me is as a woman given sight for the first time. I'm grateful that she keeps the focus on what is going on in our present; it's never necessary for us to revisit my drinking years. Yet a few times, what she needs to say to dislodge the pretty story I'd been telling myself lands like a slow-motion baseball bat in my gut.

Our work with her saves us mountains of stalemated anguish. But my ability to know what honesty feels like has atrophied like a disused muscle. I'm just discovering who I am and how to stand up for myself.

Plus, I remain haunted by T look-alikes on subways and sidewalks, even after he moves to the West Coast. These fear- and guilt-induced hallucinations do not cease until I get strong enough to get honest enough to accept my share of responsibility for the whole debacle.

"There's nothing more limiting than tapping out of tension and oversimplifying the thoughts and feelings that have the power to help us understand who we are and what we need."—Brené Brown

REBUILDING TRUST

Rebuilding trust with Bill and learning how to communicate with each other happens one conversation and situation at a time. We have a lot to learn about handling life's challenges together. We spend many awkward hours sitting side by side on the couch.

Because they change us in opposite ways, few marriages survive both the drinking and the recovery. Absence, betrayals, and lies characterize abuse of alcohol. Continuing emotional and interpersonal growth are what recovery depends on. Naturally, many partners can't adapt to this transition. But Bill and I have become closer every year.

Between Us

how sweetly your deep speaks to mine
how soft the space between us
when hearts and minds with ease incline
our silences relaxed and fine
our questions, energies align
and you've let down your last defense
how sweetly your deep speaks to mine
how soft the space between us.

FRANTIC

But during early sobriety I frequently feel frantic. Some mornings in the shower I'm desperately chanting, "God loves me unconditionally. God loves me unconditionally." It's the most comforting phrase I can think of.

The first round of holidays is to be feared. Festive ads featuring social drinking are everywhere. Everybody but you is having fun. Most alcoholics are not only haunted by the Bitch of Christmas Past, but friends and family are also leery of you and uncertain how to treat you, like whether to put a wine glass at your place setting. You have no idea how much they know about the mess you've made of your life.

I need a safe way to have a little fun. BYOL's Christmas party prompts my first sober belly laughs. One of our regulars is a supremely talented musician and comedian (and also the first bipolar person I get to know well) who leads us in renditions of sobriety carols he's written—"The Little Rummer Boy," "O J&B" [scotch], "Away in a Detox," and many more. I am one of the suitably hatted elves singing "The Twelve Steps of AA" (as in "The Twelve Days of Christmas"). Our entertainment also features a crooner singing "Have yourself a Merry AA Christmas." And of course there is a major spread of turkey dinner and desserts.

NEUROSCIENCE

Reading up on biochemistry helps me grasp what's been happening to me. By creating the sensations of desire and satiety, dopamine is evolution's way of encouraging us to do what it takes to survive. Whenever we feel pleasure or are learning something, the neurotransmitter dopamine is involved. As neuroscientist Chantel Prat explains: The amount of dopamine in the brain mix is how the brain decides if it's winning at the game of life. Not only does dopamine make you feel good, but it also creates the conditions that promote learning to help you find more of these rewards in the future. The more dopamine your brain releases, the stronger the learning.[2]

Addiction is a dysregulation of the dopamine system's reward pathways. Those who inherit a mutation of a certain dopamine receptor gene blast skyward with pleasure from their very first exposure to the substance they are vulnerable to.[3] In the brains of those who inherit this mutation or otherwise develop this dysregulation, molecules of alcohol/opioids/nicotine fit perfectly into reward receptors that keep begging for more. Also vulnerable are those whose childhoods were so painful that they're desperate for comfort.

Affected brains stop generating the neurotransmitters that regulate self-control. Recurrent desire for a single goal gouges deep ruts in the neural underpinnings of the self. Continued exposure to the substance affects billions of cells performing many functions, over time damaging several organ systems.

Emotional growth for most addicts stops when regular use begins, which is almost always before that part of the brain that comprehends risk and consequences is fully developed.

Abstaining from the substance begins the long process of denaturing our brain circuitry. Fundamental to behavior change is practicing different responses to old triggers so our brains establish new connections. The pathological patterns don't disappear, but new behaviors construct overpasses.[4]

"Consciousness is the last and latest development of the organism, and consequently also the most unfinished and weakest part of it."—Friedrich Nietzsche

---

2 Chantel Prat: *The Neuroscience of You: How Every Brain Is Different and How to Understand Yours* (Dutton, 2022).
3 Ray Kurzweil, *How to Create a Mind: The Secret of Human Thought Revealed* (Viking Penguin, 2013).
4 Marc Lewis, *The Biology of Desire: Why Addiction Is Not a Disease* (Doubleday, 2016).

RECOVERY A DAY AT A TIME

Most weekdays I show up at the noontime BYOL. I sit knitting in the front row, often the first to raise my hand as I usually relate to everything. The span of humanity frequently present includes a revered, Afroed man who, after living on the street, built a successful real estate business; an entertaining, gay art professor; a tall, handsome, uniformed cop who pretends to "check" newcomers' chips; a mystic who educates us about the gift of consciousness; plus several people with no fixed address. Some of our regulars are hilarious, and as the literature says, "We are not a glum lot." Plus there are Capitol Hill types, office workers like me, and actors, musicians, and artists. One brilliant sculptor works a piece in iron she calls "The Meeting"; it consists of rows of chairs arranged as at BYOL with only one figure present—a knitter in the front row with her head tilted as if listening intently.

EGOMANIACS WITH INFERIORITY COMPLEXES

I come to notice that intelligence can be less than helpful in staying sober. Those who pride themselves on their smarts and worldly powers have a harder time surrendering and accepting their powerlessness—one reason why addicted physicians' suicide rates are so high.[5] I'm given access to a physician-only AA meeting by the only professor at George Washington University School of Medicine who's open about being in recovery. We've met, as I'm also modestly on the faculty (facilitating an Issues in Health Care course). I've hatched the idea to hook up med students who want to learn about AA with AA members who would take them to a meeting. While this idea doesn't go anywhere, I learn a lot from my brief exposure to this generous physician.

---

5   Janet Bickel, "Drunks and Denial," *Journal of the American Medical Association* 252 (1984): 1869.

> "There are limits to how much of God's will we really want done. 'Thy will be done, but I need to keep this small thing.' This is nothing to be ashamed of, but a matter of bringing ourselves just as we are to God ... saying, 'see, this is who I am, help.'"—Gerald May, MD

What I hear at meetings continues to expand my understanding of human beings and our multiple defenses and addictions. I see how addicts drag with us a history of failed coping strategies based on avoiding reality and responsibility. A neon-lit Path of Least Resistance beckons—it's so much easier to give up and give in, as in "once a loser, always a loser." This conclusion is typical of egomaniacs with inferiority complexes. Alcoholism breeds staggering self-absorption. We become inventive liars and drama queens (adrenaline rush!). Most of us could teach a master class in pretending.

Simply removing alcohol does not cure self-will run riot. Plus, we push away our loved ones and those who try to help. How could anybody love or depend on someone who is reliably their own worst enemy? When asked about the saddest thing she'd ever seen, Mother Teresa replied, "The loneliness of the alcoholic."

> "We are always becoming the self our most recent choice calls into being."—William Egginton

MY REWORKING OF KEY STEPS

Since AA's 1935 founding, a great deal has been learned about facilitating behavior change. AA's anachronistic literature does not reflect these insights and remains riddled with male pronouns and unhelpful terms. Nonetheless, as a practical and spiritual guide, the program works for those who find community within it.

Step three, "Made a decision to turn our life and our will over to the care of God as we understood Him," stymies many, because who knows what "turning our will over to God" looks like? I figure that going to meetings and staying sober show I made the right decision.

"What we need is to love without getting tired."—Mother Teresa

PERSONAL INVENTORY

And I really need to get on with step four's "searching and fearless moral inventory." The terms "fearless" and "moral," however, are not helpful. All alcoholics bring sources of shame and fear into this examination that resist the light of naming.

I'd begun concluding that unless Bill became radically easier to live with, I was either going to drink again or to leave again. This, I come to learn, is the Gift of Desperation and not to be wasted. After my far-from-thorough first pass at step five (that is, sharing my inventory, in this case with my pastor), most importantly, I stay sober. And this work better equips me to accept life on life's terms, including people. Also, the boxing gloves with the program that I hadn't known I was wearing, drop off. A triple win for me.

"Irritation is the dark underside of love."—Linda Pastan

When I am ready for a more thorough step five with a sponsor, we focus on the fears that might make me drink again and on what's hardest about staying sober. She assures me that there's nothing special about any of the degrading mistakes I made under the influence and that I can join the human race in recovery. It feels like thorns being pulled out of my heart. I can't stop smiling the rest of the day.

In Praise of Truth

the story of your life to tell
what's real may want to hide away
your fears you fiercely try to quell
you never on a darkness dwell
arriving from your shadowed well
your truth is eager for her say
the story of your life to tell
what's real you must not hide away.

Steps six and seven unhelpfully state, "Were entirely ready to have God remove all these defects of character," and "Humbly asked Him to remove our shortcomings." Instead of "defects of character," I focus on *self-centered fears*, which we're helpfully told fall into two categories—fears we'll lose something we already have, and fears we'll fail to get something we feel we deserve. I begin looking these fears in the face. As I stop feeling ashamed of them, they lessen, bit by bit.

These steps get me started on the delayed work of figuring out where I'm stuck with one foot on the brake and the other on the gas, how I get in my own way, and what to take responsibility for without causing more problems. I'm finally teachable.

"My own heart let me have more pity on."—Gerard Manley Hopkins

MARRIAGE IS A MIRACLE

Lessons from my experience do not automatically dawn on me. I need Carmen's continuing help.

So does Bill. We've only been back together for two years when his beloved father dies. In addition to his own grief, now and for many years his mother in St. Louis needs much more from him. Simultaneously, he's just striking out on his own as a graphic designer.

For a while, the number of adjustments seems overwhelming. Carmen offers the analogy of a mobile, a structure so balanced that it turns freely in the air. When either spouse adds a big deal (illness, job loss, death, etc.) to the family mobile, it gets out of whack. Slowly Bill and I get better at rebalancing ours. Carmen reminds us: "Marriage is a Miracle."

> "All loving is the skillful harmonizing of asymmetries across the scales of personhood and preferences between ... two separate consciousnesses, each half-opaque to itself."—Alain de Botton

THE GIFT

Just as empathy depends on neural processes that change only gradually, Alcoholics Anonymous is a slow delivery system. Impatience is an unaffordable argument with reality. Minimizing arguments with plaid realities makes it easier to stay sober.

Service work is also critical. For me, this means participating in my weekly virtual women's meeting, as well as program chairing, leading meetings when asked, and sponsoring.

At its best, Alcoholics Anonymous is a gift that is an *agent of change*. Lewis Hyde writes that the spirit of such a gift is kept alive only by its constant donation: "It is only when the gift has worked in us, only when we have come up to its level, that we can give it away again. Passing the gift along is the act of gratitude that finishes the labor."[6] Hence, a pain becomes a medicine—a lock, a key—and a vulnerability, a source of abundance.

Hammock

=offline	unplugged
=supine	beneath
a canopy	of greens
sunlit	or shade
depending on	the breeze
asway	I gaze
at butterflies	and bees
and slip inside	cicada timpani
and crickets' strings	and katydiddiddids—
all safely hid	in summer heaven

---

6 Lewis Hyde, *The Gift: Creativity and the Artist in the Modern World* (Vintage, 2007).

PART II

STRIVING

CHAPTER 5

LEADING WOMEN IN MEDICINE AND STARTING A BUSINESS

One day at a time, my judgment and professionalism improve.

LOTS OF ISSUES

I develop colleagueships with many more constituents—in addition to medical students, now deans of admissions, student affairs, and financial aid. After working with these deans from almost every medical school, I realize that, thanks to Brown's start-up, I have a greater breadth of experience in medical education than anyone I meet.

Working with the women student affairs deans also teaches me about the needs of the first large wave of women medical students and the massive, but as yet ignored, institutional barriers they face.

AFFIRMATION

On my departure from directing AAMC's student organization, the representatives passed this resolution:

"In our frantic lives as medical students we all too often find ourselves frustrated but unable to express frustration and committed but wavering in our ability to manifest commitment. Occasionally, we encounter a special person who can help us elucidate those feelings, which we have difficulty sorting through. With such a person we can evolve to a greater awareness of our common needs, as students and as human beings. Janet Bickel is such a person."

With excellent timing, as I am ready for a new challenge, in 1987 the new AAMC president sees the wisdom of funding an Office of Women in Medicine. For the first time in history, sexual discrimination and harassment are in the news, and the deans are noticing how very male they are. AAMC suddenly needs somebody who knows anything about gender-related subjects. I am perfectly situated to direct the new office.

INSTITUTIONAL BARRIERS

The issues facing women professionals have been accruing since they were allowed into universities. I am deluged with hair-raising accounts of every kind of humiliation. Women from all specialties and levels report being ignored if they are not likeable or attractive but propositioned if a bit too likeable and attractive; being groped in elevators and even operating rooms; finding slides of *Playboy* covers inserted into lectures devoid of content pertaining to women's health; receiving salaries thousands of dollars below those of male peers ("Doesn't your husband make plenty?"); being left off the list of co-authors; rarely being introduced as "doctor"; facing difficulties gaining nurses' respect and secretarial assistance; being talked over in meetings where they seldom get full credit for their ideas; being excluded from departmental social activities built around basketball, golf, hunting, and fishing; being expected to work until their due date and be back at work after a month of "sick" leave, and good luck finding extended-hour childcare or space to nurse an infant.

At the intersection of two caste systems, women of color report the most dehumanizing experiences.[7]

---

7   Isabel Wilkerson, *Caste: The Origins of Our Discontents* (Random House, 2020).

"To describe the world more fully is to change it."—Edith Wharton

Emerging from eons of isolation, women begin to pool their experiences. They discover how dysfunctional, durable, and inhumane is much of the established order. Women notice how easily white men translate whatever intellectual capital they have into career capital and how oblivious they are to the privileges they inherit by virtue of genetic luck alone, as if they earned these privileges forever in a fair fight at the dawn of time. Some women get sidetracked by resentment. But anything that interferes with agility or with building allies is unaffordable.

ACTION

I begin by introducing myself to the few women leaders I can identify who are well-positioned to guide program planning. These are women who have made it in a man's world without sacrificing their health or values and who are keen to lend their expertise.

I use every means possible to strengthen the role of the Women's Liaison Officers appointed by each medical school, including publishing statistics ranking each school on such variables as the proportion of full professors who are women. I author a book[8] and numerous scholarly articles[9] and a newsletter.

Whenever possible, I connect with women leaders of the medical, scientific, and higher education professional societies that are organizing to recruit and advance women in their fields, and I connect them to each other. I seek out improvements in childcare in hospitals, salary equity, and mentoring programs, and publish them as resources.

---

8   *Women in Medicine: Getting In, Growing, and Advancing* (Sage Publications, 2000).
9   Beginning with "Women in Medical Education: A Status Report" in *The New England Journal of Medicine* 319 (1988):1579–84, which put our office on the national map. My boss, Joseph Keyes, JD, encouraged me to submit my manuscript to this prestigious journal, but if NEJM's deputy editor, Marcia Angell, MD, had not fought for it, it would've been rejected.

Naturally we change agents discover that, with so little standing in these competitive hierarchies, women can do little to effect necessary reforms; e.g., implementing humanistic parental leave policies. We make a strong case that these changes will improve the culture for everybody, prevent loss of talent, and be good for business.[10] But it's powerful men with lots of other pressing agendas who are going to have to lead these changes. Where is this wisdom to be found?

> "Curiosity might be pictured as made up of chains of small questions extending outwards ... encompassing more and more of the world until at some point we may reach that elusive stage where we are bored by nothing."—Alain de Botton

CAREER AND LEADERSHIP DEVELOPMENT PROGRAMS

My most significant contribution becomes career and leadership development programs for women faculty. Previously, AAMC sponsored programs only for deans, hospital CEOs, and department heads, so extending services to individual faculty represents a stretch. For these three-day programs, women leaders from around the country share their expertise with promising younger colleagues. Workshops cover financial management, negotiating, public speaking, and other key skills that men learn from mentors.

As most of these women have given up other passions for the sake of their families and careers, I also offer evening discussions titled "Do you know where your creativity is?" I encourage attendees to share examples of what creativity means to them at this point. Many relate poignant stories—one wins a state fly-fishing contest but doesn't tell anyone at work; one's toddler leads her toward the piano because mommy is always happy there; one sponsors dinners where her graduate students cook their native cuisine.

---

10   J. Bickel, D. Wara, B.F. Atkinson, L. S. Cohen, M. Dunn, S. Hostler, T. Johnson, P. Morahan, A.H. Rubenstein, G.F. Sheldon, and E. Stokes, "Increasing Women's Leadership in Academic Medicine: Report of the AAMC Project Implementation Committee," *Academic Medicine* 77 (2002):1043–61.

Many participants tell me, "I'll never again feel so lonely." In later years, after almost every talk I give, a woman approaches me with "Your program made all the difference in my getting promoted." These programs, moreover, serve as a model for AAMC's subsequent minority faculty career development programs and for some professional societies.[11][12]

> "Could you tell me how to grow—or is it unconveyed—like Melody—or Witchcraft?"—Emily Dickinson

PERFORMANCE PRESSURES

Many women's expectations of what AAMC's office can do are unrealistic, exacerbating the heavy performance pressure I've been applying to myself from the start, continually plowing unplowed ground. I'm developing colleagues at almost every medical school in North America, but I have no real partners, except for my loyal and kind administrative assistant.

With no experience in delegating, I bungle the management of the first staff assistant I'm allowed. I don't know how to create a space safe enough for her to ask me the questions necessary for our work together to proceed. I develop a functional partnership with the second one, although I regularly grow resentful of her lack of help writing our newsletter, despite the convincing evidence she's provided that she cannot write.

BEYOND WOMEN IN MEDICINE AND SCIENCE

From my start at AAMC, I introduce myself to and encourage constituents to tell me about what's going on at their schools that we might help them

---

11 D. Helitzer, S.L. Newbill, P. Morahan, D. Magrane, et al., "Perceptions of Skill Development of Participants in Three National Development Programs for Women Faculty in Academic Medicine," *Academic Medicine* 89 (2014): 896–903.
12 The subsequent establishment of the Executive Leadership in Academic Medicine (ELAM) Program for Women fellowship created a track whereby numerous women physicians and scientists have progressed into leadership roles. See R. Jagsi and N.D. Spector, "Leading by Design: Lessons for the Future from 25 Years of the Executive Leadership in Academic Medicine (ELAM) Program for Women," *Academic Medicine* 95 (October 2020):1479–1482.

address. And I study all the medical education journals for promising directions and introduce myself to the lead authors to learn more. Out of these seemingly obvious strategies, I initiate many additional firsts. I pull together a conference of ethicists, medical professors, residency program directors, student affairs deans, residents, and students to share strategies for assisting trainees to deal with encroaching ethical compromises (e.g., your attending shows up drunk, or you're told to lie to a patient),[13] fueling an emerging focus on student professionalism.

I investigate medical schools' parental leave policies, changes in tenure policies, part-time faculty promotion policies, and emerging HIV/AIDS curricula, publishing the first national studies of these. I program the first AAMC annual meeting focus on gay and lesbian health issues. A senior staffer complains that this is "too political." I respond, "No focus at all is just as political." When faculty affairs deans approach AAMC for help, I'm the first staff member to listen; this focus grows into a new professional development group.

No one else at the association seems interested in any of this low-hanging fruit. I take every advantage of my autonomy.

Throughout these years, I'm connecting people across disciplines, institutions, roles, and castes. It never occurs to me to think of myself as a leader. The opportunities present as mine to do, so I do my best.

SWALLOWING DISAPPOINTMENT AND DETACHING

When my boss moves me to an office with no view of the sky (to give his favored guy space to expand), I have a really hard time adjusting. Window-addicted, I just can't stay indoors on nice afternoons. I take walks, often buying an ice cream cone, and gain ten pounds.

---

13 "Human Values Teaching Programs in the Clinical Education of Medical Students," *Journal of Medical Education* 62 (1987): 369–78; and *Educating for Professionalism: Creating a Culture of Humanism in Medical Education* (University of Iowa Press, 2000), co-edited with Delese Wear.

So even though my job appears enviable, I occasionally look at other possibilities. The first National Institutes of Health office dedicated to women's health research is just gearing up.[14] I interview with Dr. Ruth Kirschstein for a possible role in this new office. She helps me see that I would have far less scope within the NIH bureaucracy than I enjoy at AAMC.

The professional society I'm most active in welcomes my interest in becoming its next executive director. Since I seem to be a perfect fit for this, losing out teaches me a hard lesson. With my ego fused to this exciting possibility, I was incapable of objectivity; clearly the other candidate's business expertise made him a much better fit at that juncture.

None of the AAMC bigwigs express any interest in the report I first author, representing five years of a task force's work on how to increase women's leadership. I'm used to swallowing disappointment. Once the AAMC president called me into his office to object to my inviting someone from the NIH Women's Health Research Office to discuss the inclusion of women in clinical trials. Staring at my legs, he questions the value of this NIH office, given that he himself had excelled at caring for women as well as men in his former practice.

"Patriarchy that spared me / fame."—Maxine Kumin

Even more dismaying: Our big Women in Medicine and Science luncheon is the only annual event attended by the AAMC chairman, who sits at the head table. Hillary Clinton has just given a standing-room-only speech on health care reform.

---

14 Prior to this, government-funded clinical trials were not required to include women. Differences between the bodies of men and women were considered too tricky to study and therefore irrelevant. This Office of Women's Health Research owed its start to the late Dr. Ruth Kirschstein, the first woman to direct any NIH institute and who twice served as NIH Deputy Director. As a medical student at Brown, Ruth's son, Arnold Rabson, became my friend and introduced me to his truly wonderful parents (Dr. Alan Rabson was a beloved longtime senior leader of the National Cancer Institute).

I turn to this year's self-satisfied executive: "Lance, what was your takeaway from Clinton's presentation?"

"With those legs she should never wear a skirt that length."

Everyone pretends he didn't say this. Responding effectively to a man who oozes carefree superiority while dumbfounding you with his backwardness takes practice. You want to construct a reply that teaches him a lesson without his losing any face. Self-confidence, political savvy, and excellent timing are necessary to know when to spread sugar and when to "throw sharp elbows."[15] Hell hath no fury like a man devalued, so most people choose silence as the safer option.

> "Sometimes it is better to be a little ashamed rather than silent."
> —Czeslaw Milosz

Prove That You Are Not a Chatbot

What does it mean to be fully alive?
    At what point does contentment become
    both a positive trait and a possibility?

    How is it that our passions choose us
    rather than the other way around?

Describe the last time you changed your mind.
These days how would you describe a normal life?

    We give our harshest critics rent-free inner space.
    Why does no one naturally befriend herself?

---

15 Thanks to *Washington Post* critic-in-chief Robin Givhan for singling out Nancy Pelosi for "broadening the vocabulary of what it means to throw sharp elbows."

Discuss these lines from the poet Naomi Shihab Nye:
"Before you can know kindness as the deepest thing inside,
you must know sorrow as the other deepest thing."

Will humans ever embrace their own diversity?
How much can we expect men to understand about the history of
women?
What does history teach about the powerful purposely reducing
their own power?

Why is the world
so beautiful?

PUBLIC SPEAKING

Besides sitting still in windowless rooms, another critical skill I lack is speaking before groups. Even reporting the results of my master's research to a small group of interested students, I am undone. My hands tremble so badly I can't read my notes (like in seventh grade when I'm asked to play the piano for our morning hymn, and my right leg develops a convulsive life of its own). In my second attempt at a podium, I begin without an organizing outline, surprised that the repetitive rereading of my notes was insufficient preparation. I don't know how to prepare or get help.

My first major talk at a medical school feels disastrous. I'm speaking to an audience of primarily male physicians who don't quite believe gender equity is a valid subject for their attention. My first slide is upside down (in olden times—i.e., before PowerPoint in 1992—we labored over carousels, which malfunctioned in many ways even when the presenter correctly arranged her slides). Compounding my humiliation, I blurt out that my husband had doublechecked my slides for me.

After my first talk at a conference at which my boss is present, he recommends, "Maybe if you try imagining yourself as an actor, you can project more confidence." While I can't explain that I've been holding back tears all week from the cyclical breast pain that renders even showering uncomfortable, this feedback spurs me to contact a speech pathologist, who teaches me to make better use of my vocal apparatus and breath.

So the next time I'm being introduced and my heart starts racing, I know to inhale as deeply as I can and then to seriously lengthen my exhale, relaxing the diaphragm; this works. Additional breakthroughs occur when I start forcing myself to practice in front of a mirror. Also emboldening are pushups. As typically the only person in the auditorium without a doctorate, I have to work extra hard to be credible.

GRADUAL IMPROVEMENTS

I gradually get better at using visuals and speaking with minimal notes. Yet after one talk, an attendee asks, "Are you aware of how many 'umms' you insert?" Until I tape myself, I don't believe her. Oh God. Something else to work on. I take advantage of an expert educator's offer to videotape me and debrief the tape—a big help.

Presentation skills coaches recommend sticking to a few main points. But I am continuously integrating new findings into my presentations and am jealous of stand-up comics who never introduce more than one new bit at a time into a routine, honing it over several tries.

With my audiences of medical academics, I'm unlikely to get another chance. Men don't generally find the paucity of women leaders to be a problem. Occasionally a powerful guy stands up and manufactures an aggressive joke. The unmentioned targets of their animosity are the women who invited me to speak.

Over time I, and my audiences, improve.

Me at podium

When things go well, how sweet is the achievement of getting somewhere new together.

A few times I am brought in, I later see, as window dressing. If a dean can point to having a national expert speak or consult on gender issues, he might get credit for doing something, as if lip service were better than nothing. Data on the economic value of supporting women's career development (attrition is very costly) and on strategies to accomplish this do not convince those who prefer to assume that women with children are incapable of building a productive academic career, so why bother to mentor them. If a woman is so ambitious and brilliant that you can't help but encourage her, but then she has the nerve to become a source of competition, you can drop her, in a stroke dramatically reducing her influence.

With women audiences, exchanges are much more educational and productive. Women ask shared questions that lead to useful dialogues, often of a kind unlikely to occur in male-dominant groups—how to get credit for ideas, develop confidence, negotiate for maternity leave, gain the cooperation of a secretary/nurse/mentor/partner. How to get a RAISE!

A WAKE-UP CALL

In 2001, on the last night of a vacation spent snorkeling, I dream that I am knitting two enormous bedspreads and that it doesn't make sense to be working on both simultaneously.[16]

Then in the dream I'm in a church basement, where an older woman is demonstrating a way of weaving in natural materials like feathers, fossils, shells, pebbles, leaves. I have never been so fascinated by anything in my life. I ask how much the tools and materials cost; the sum is astronomical.

My Fish Story

On our pond I launch a boat
    and ply a hook
    and fish alone—
    three firsts.

---

16 Knitting has great significance to me: as an aid to sitting still and staying present, as a way of working with color, and most especially as a way to create slippers as gifts to friends. Knitting also connects me with my grandmothers, who did not sit down without some handiwork in their laps.

I would celebrate these victories—
    stay fixed on blackbirds' serenade and zip of damselflies
    and snag a fish.
Instead, some barbed old hurt snags me
    and races far away from this here day.

Rescued by a little bass
    who open-eyed endures my battle with the barb—
pliers rescue both.

In bed my mind still flickers
    high above those cattails, muddy shore—
    beyond my caring whether this
    has all been writ before.

FAREWELL

As I awaken, I recognize the woman in the dream as my wise older self. I must quit my job. My extreme preference for time outdoors and other freedoms cannot be joined to having a boss and office hours, too many of which are spent in meetings where I'm not learning or contributing anything. Since I've stopped growing in directions of importance to me, I risk more by staying than by leaping into the unknown.

I'm leaving behind a substantial salary and benefits, security, national status and, finally, a corner office. What I actually end up missing the most about working at the national level are opportunities to connect people with resources and with each other.

At a farewell lunch, a long-time AAMC colleague says, "I know you won't want to hear this, but you've been a negative influence in many staff meetings because you often appear disengaged" (having ceased knitting in meetings, I am usually subtly working on something more meaningful to me). This important feedback reveals to me how I have defaulted on my responsibilities to other group members—a critical lesson in group dynamics for me.

AFFIRMATIONS

On my departure from AAMC, I receive many tributes and thank-yous. I am referred to as "Janet Appleseed" and as a leader who has "knit together" hundreds of people. Even the deans pass a resolution in my honor. One colleague helps me see my lack of peers as a strength rather than a deficit: "You are a person who is her own model, her own teacher, and has not needed a reference group. I see a woman of her own creation whose destiny comes from within."

STARTING A BUSINESS

After a year spent trying out various ways of framing my expertise and reading every potential resource I can find, in 2003 I leap into the then bleeding-edge field of coaching academic physicians and scientists. I've been doing all I can to get the word out about my availability as a coach and consultant. But conflict of interest policies prohibit my mentioning my services unless asked. And I discover that most of my academic colleagues distrust consultants and now steer clear of me. So initially I have very few clients. On the first morning in my home office, I irrationally feel as if I do not deserve breakfast because "He who does not work, neither shall he eat." Isn't this sad? I blame Martin Luther.

Tellingly, my much fiddled-over business mission statement focuses only on what I hope to give to my clients and on how I hope to grow. Absent is making a living! After creating a website and business stationery and becoming certified to administer the Myers-Briggs Type Indicator and a multi-rater feedback instrument, I am rather at a loss. No wonder I'm often sleepless. I don't even know what to charge.

I have five colleagues with established coaching/consulting practices whom I count as friends and whose careers I've helped. Naturally I'm hoping they'll share insights with me. Instead, four stop responding to me (I'd worked very closely with one person for almost twenty years). If they were viewing me as competition, they were wrong. It's taken me two decades to see that it was their insecurity that occasioned their dropping me.

THE HARD WAY

So I learn the practice of coaching the hard way—on my own, again. Enrolling in a coach training program would've helped a lot, although there weren't many to pick from at the time. I did not pursue this option, naively overrelying on the advice of one of my "friends."

Another unpredicted difficulty is how many of my early clients are remedial—sent by bosses who are making one last documentable attempt before terminating them. I gradually see that my biggest failure with these clients is not recognizing earlier that their problems are not coachable—their blind spots are too big, the environments they are trapped in are too toxic, and/or they need therapy. I do no one any favors by continuing to try to help. But I don't feel like I can say no to business.

DIE OF SHAME?

A workshop led by educator Robert Kegan, PhD, offers a crucial insight. His work facilitates uncovering what's going on when we've got one foot on the gas and the other on the brake. He offers a framework for seeing what assumptions are getting in the way of our acting on our stated commitments and for testing the validity of these assumptions and discovering what fears they reveal.[17] I see that one of my assumptions is that if I fail to build a successful business, I will die of shame. Holy cow—I need to lighten up!

On the train home from a conference where none of my interactions with potential clients go anywhere, from the window I notice a fisherman checking his lines. If no fish bite, he's obviously not going to blame himself. I stop feeling quite so inadequate.

Fairly easily I get used to being my own secretary (counting it a business write-off, I buy myself flowers on Secretary's Day, as they used to call it). But without tech support I suffer intensely from computer insecurity, and because of phone issues I'm clueless about, I'm often straining to hear clients.

At a nonmedical leadership conference, I facilitate a session for coaches to discuss our stresses. We draw images of ourselves as a coach. My crude drawing shows a figure hunched over a vegetable garden, sweating profusely as I struggle to interpret each plant's needs, as none come with plant tags.

Gradually my coaching improves and my practice builds.

SPEAKING AT 125 ACADEMIC HEALTH CENTERS

Over the past thirty years, 125 North American academic health centers (AHCs) have invited me to offer leadership coaching and career development sessions. I usually invite my hosts to book me up for two full days. Since I drink a lot of water, I must have visited more different hospital bathrooms than anybody in the world. Such heavy scheduling maximizes my opportunities for engaging with faculty and leaders, but the performance pressures are extreme. As I abhor gyms, my only stress-relief valve is walking as fast and long as I can manage (in parking lots if necessary—best are university campuses). By the time I'm being driven to the airport, I am sometimes vibrating with total interpersonal exhaustion.

I have a lot to learn about trusting and pacing myself.

---

17 Robert Kegan and Lisa Laskow Lahey, *Immunity to Change: How to Overcome It and Unlock the Potential in Yourself and Your Organization* (Harvard Business School Press, 2009).

Flying

Clouds floating by above
calm me down
as I await my Uber.

I'm TSA-Precheck
but my airline forgets and ejects me
into the long digestive track of a line.
Finally I get to remove my shoes.

After waiting for a gate for half an hour
a wonky jet bridge adds another.
The hysterical toddler ratchets up her screams—
"I need my mommy right NOW! I need my mommy right NOW!"
Don't we all.

Delays cascade across the East.
A determined array of hips and bellies races from gate to gate
hauling wheeled attachments, caged pets
babies on fronts and backs and ferried.

Hour after airport hour, lines sprout everywhere
and we are exhausted, exasperated
bored off our tits and stir-crazy.

Yet not one mean word do I hear—
perhaps we rabble are salvageable
and will survive our plagues, delays, and babels.

RELATIONAL COMMUNICATION

Greatly facilitating my continuing evolution, Penny Williamson[18] invites me to participate in her Courage to Lead program. Based on the work of distinguished educator Parker Palmer, in circles of trust formed over five quarterly retreats, a group of ten explores significant choice points in our lives; our crucibles (i.e., the trials that change us); our birthright gifts and which of these are at the heart of our lives and work, and how we express and sometimes overuse them. We learn to hold tension rather than running from it and how, when the going gets tough, to turn to wonder (as in "I wonder what is going on with her.") Each person has the opportunity to be the focus of a Clearness Committee, wherein she describes an issue or dilemma near the center of her life to a few people intent on asking open questions, inviting the focus person to thereby access her own wisdom. We come to be able to describe ourselves in a freshly accurate, kind, and often humorous way without reference to any label or comparison.

At the program's close, we're invited to write in each other's retreat journals. I collect: "You are honest about your struggles in a way that helps me with my own"; "You give so much of your whole self at every turn"; "I saw glimpses of the girl within who'll never stop longing to learn more"; and "Trust yourself." This supportive naming waters my driest roots.

I begin to notice a paradox: I crave affirmation, yet remain unable to fully internalize, to truly benefit from, what I receive. Is this because I haven't sufficiently proved my worth to *myself?* What's going on here?

At these retreats during frequent walks on Cape Cod's rocky beach, I come to see how lonely this striver has been for her whole life, how lacking in peer companionship. I've been hauling boulders of responsibilities on

---

18 Penny Williamson, ScD, internationally recognized facilitator, educator, coach, and founding mentor with the national Center for Courage and Renewal arrives at exactly the right time to become my teacher.

my back—while expecting myself to be shouldering ever more weight—all with no partner or guide.

That I grew up on Mentor Place used to feel unfair. Reflecting now on how many have benefited from my scholarship, coaching, and programs, this street name feels predictive, strengthening. And I'm reminded of the Mother's Day card Linda sent me, celebrating all the nurture I've given our nieces and nephews and their kids and our godchildren and my AA sponsees and the many I've coached. Along with pebbles, the tide washes away some of my rocks of self-judgment and insecurity.

EMOTIONAL INTELLIGENCE

During this interval, I'm also studying for certification to administer an instrument that assesses emotional intelligence.[19] The intelligent use of our emotions in relationships can be described as the ability to identify our feelings as they arise, to connect our personal experiences with those of others, and to remain open and centered even when we feel devalued and challenged.

Assuming I would score high, when my results indicate that I have a lot to work on, I question the test's validity. But the course soon shows me how much room I have to grow; after all, for most of my life I suppressed my fears. I learn that I have much greater access to negative than to positive emotions and that I am more likely to arrive at a negative than a constructive interpretation of a difficult situation. During stressful interactions I tend to lose trust in both myself and in others, rather than asking myself for evidence of whether this loss of trust is warranted. And when focusing on another person, I easily lose touch with my own needs and experience, rather than keeping a balance between myself and the other person.

---

19 For more on emotional intelligence, see chapter 4 of my book *Equip Your Inner Coach: Personal, Career, and Leadership Development in an Uncertain Age* (2022). The instrument I become certified in displays videotaped scenarios depicting tense boss/employee conflicts followed by questions eliciting responses to the scenarios. http://learninginaction.com/services/EI-in-action-profile/EI-in-action-profile-assessment/

One easily initiated practice supports growth in emotional intelligence: Whenever I notice my heart speeding up or another visceral clue, I pause and ask myself, "What hooked me? Why am I reacting so strongly?" When I pause, I always notice something useful. My ability to learn from the information contained in my negative emotions quickly improves. This mindfulness helps me notice my defenses as they arise, so I can gently ask what I am defending myself against and why. Soon I'm attuning to others more accurately and with much less strain as well.

LEADING ORGANIZATIONS TO HEALTH

With Penny's encouragement, I enroll in the Leading Organizations to Health program.[20] This brilliantly designed series walks a small group of leaders through carefully mediated steps supporting them to, within the space of hours, work closely together in very interpersonally challenging ways. This program demonstrates what a group of people can achieve— and the fun they can have together—once trust is built. We learn to notice how our communication patterns shape outcomes and how to improve these, and how the way we show up influences others, and what authentic presence feels like.[21]

An indelible learning arrives when my program coach interrupts me, exclaiming, "JANET JANET JANET, do you hear how HARD you're being on yourself?" This startling confirmation of my continuing knee-jerk harsh self-judgment advances my ability to notice it and to substitute sympathy.

Comments collected in my retreat journal:

"Your growing calm moves me to my core, to see you relaxing into the present with great vitality"; "How you notice nature influenced all of us,

---

20 Led by Anthony L. Suchman, MD, and Diane Rawlins, Relationship-Centered Health Care Principles; https://www.aamc.org/career-development/leadership-development/leading-organizations-health
21 Nicole A. Steckler, Diane Rawlins, Penelope Williamson, and Anthony L. Suchman, "Preparing to Lead Change: An Innovative Curriculum Integrating Theory, Group Skills and Authentic Presence," *Healthcare* 4 (2016): 247–251.

and you also made us more literate"; and "You make us ask bigger questions of ourselves."

Being held in these circles of trust brings to the fore my central question and its answer: If I'm not striving, who am I? I am sufficient being who I am right now—a beloved child of my parents and of God and of the Earth. The striver can begin to learn how to relax—a plateau is in view. Huzzah!

These retreats also inspire and enable me to design and facilitate opportunities for people to teach each other how to more effectively work together.[22] Modeling courageous presence and relying on inquiry and generative listening, I'm equipped to turn differences and tensions into learning opportunities.

I finally hit my stride as an educator. It only took a lifetime, and it's easy to get out of practice.

CAREER SUMMARY

At the best possible points in my development, and completely unplanned, I arrived first at a surefire start-up grounding me in a very broad and useful knowledge base, and then at the ideal organization for putting my expertise to use, one that allowed me as much autonomy as I could use.

Another amazing stroke of luck: I couldn't have chosen better constituents than medical students and women health care professionals and scientists—with their energetic commitment to service, wide-ranging intelligence, and underdog status. It's only a slight exaggeration to say that I always felt privileged to be learning from and partnering with them.

Anyone who gets to work out of her strengths and values for any extended period and take home fair recompense has been fantastically fortunate—and I've had fifty years and counting.

---

22 Alexandra Suchman (CEO, BarometerXP), a colleague from this Relationship-Centered Health Care program, has designed innovative games to develop facilitation and team skills. https://www.barometerxp.com

I've been further advantaged by the support of a multitalented husband who's never doubted my abilities ("Oh, you always get As") nor shown too much interest, thank heaven, in my work.

These boons have enabled me to become the architect of my own life.

> "The larger loneliness of our lives evolves from our unwillingness to spend ourselves, stir ourselves."—Carol Shields

PROGRESS?

In terms of legal and political standing, in my grandmother's era, women and people of color barely existed. Thus, compared to the preceding millenniums, progress in the last century has been swift. My goddaughters have a hundred times more women role models than I had.

On the other hand, for the first time in twenty years, the percentage of executives who are women has declined below twelve percent. The number of Fortune 500 CEOs who are women only barely exceeds the number whose name is "John."

Of much greater concern is that, even in countries in which women can vote, *human rights* that women presumed they had wrested from history are being taken away. Fueling this backlash is an obdurate *unconscious fear of women's power* on the part of men and women who consider themselves rational. Working free of this fear begins only when denial of it ends.

Yet *despite* the hundreds of women leaders I know, the word "doctor" still elicits in me a masculine image. That I'll never be completely free of associating authority with the male sex appalls me—and educates me and emboldens me for the never-ending work of upgrading our models of power and of leadership. I take comfort in the possibility that I've contributed to how today's young women tend to be far more tuned in to their bodies, rights, goals, and needs than my generation was at their age. Across age groups, we all ought to be doing more to cheer each other on in this work of humanizing the world.

> "Learn to think for a long time how to change this world, how to make it better to live in. All the people in the world ought to talk about it."—Quetzalcoatl

People-nurturers and people-connectors are invested in an *infinite* game—that is, growing in freedoms and uniqueness in concert with others—in contrast to finite competitions for money and power.[23] We're planting seeds, nurturing them, adapting to the crappy soil we inherited. We can't guess which seeds will root and thrive and produce more seeds and which of these will bloom. As author Annie Ernaux wrote, "One cannot see the future of something learned."

---

23   James Carse, *Finite and Infinite Games: A Vision of Life as Play and Possibility* (Ballantine Books, 1986).

WE'RE PUT HERE TO LOVE

CHAPTER 6

INHABITING MY BODY

"How easy and natural love is if you are well!"—Jonathan Franzen

UNIVERSAL RENT

Pain is the universal rent for having a body, so why dwell on it?

Another argument against this chapter is that each person's perceptions of and frame of reference for her body's heavens and hells and how she processes visceral clues are unique, variable, and to a large extent unable to be shared. Cycles of suffering and of flourishing may overlap in ways impossible to pin down.

Moreover, establishing causality is often impossible given the entanglement of our body parts and the interdependencies of our physical, cognitive, emotional, and spiritual selves, not to mention our unconscious and archetypal intelligences.

And yet, hidden as they often are from view, our body's peculiarities and disabilities determine so much about what happens.

MY HEALTHY BODY

As is true for everyone, I beat stupefying odds against being conceived. I bow to my parents in thanks for the healthy constitutions that my siblings and I inherited. Even with deteriorating knees, last year Brian and I achieved a climb from 10,500 to 12,500 feet in the Colorado Rockies.

Nothing beats hiking in the mountains for that sense of unbounded and motor-free space that I crave. Plus, what fun to be fist-bumped by young people for "crunchin' it!" I chuckle that at 75 I can still do the "happy laughing baby" pose in yoga.

As an ephemeral aggregation of atoms, some of which may've passed through a lichen, I'm grateful that my ecosystems of microscopic communities generally get along so well with each other and with my surroundings.

My reliable energy is a boon, but I don't get sleepy easily. Wakefulness some nights and early mornings seems natural. I'm lucky that eating vegetables and exercising are good for me because I would do that anyway.

FEMALE

My luck did not extend to hormones. After a late start, at fifteen my estrogen comes on strong—quick increases in breast size, appetite, and weight. The only thing I can think to cut out is the margarine on my toast. Ice cream is too much of a comfort. I battle a stubborn fifteen to twenty extra pounds for most of the next many decades. Especially after giving up cigarettes, food uncomfortably dominates my consciousness. I often long for an appetite-suppressant.[24]

I become aware of a disturbing disjunction. The more feminine I look and the more care I take with my appearance, the more unwelcome eyes I draw—even as, inside, I'm the same person.

BIRTH CONTROL

In 1979, highly publicized research revealed that women on birth control pills who smoke substantially increase their chances of lung cancer.

---

24 I confessed these difficulties to Carmen, who said: "As you become more self-directed and keep following your interests, your appetite will move off center stage." And it did. What a relief after being so preoccupied with food for so long. Then, during the pandemic, suffering six months of cyst-on-spinal-nerve sciatica disappeared fifteen pounds.

We smokers are made to feel like idiots if we keep taking the pill. And drinking without smoking? Unimaginable, no matter how hard Bill lobbies for me to quit.

We decide on a vasectomy. He's inclined in this direction, having concluded that he'd never be as good a father as his dad was and that my continued use of the pill would be harmful to me in the long run.

Once I quit drinking at age thirty-three, severe PMS sets in. Dives in confidence send me to my closet, where I sit and cry. Vitamin B12 and increasing sobriety help. Also troubling, my cycles become wildly volatile—spaced 20, then 50, then 35, then 60 days apart.

At age thirty-nine I become emotionally healthy enough to imagine motherhood for the first time. I've been inspired by the many thriving professionals at the conferences I host who are happy parents. After some heartfelt discussion and a few brief bouts of depression, with Bill's support, a feeling of rightness returns that not becoming parents was the best decision for us.

BREAST PAIN

Sometimes for two weeks per cycle, breast tenderness intensifies to acute mastalgia. Fresh from a refresher course, my gynecologist suggests a hysterectomy; I can't tell if she's serious. We discuss an androgen—a male sex hormone. She warns of facial hair and permanent voice deepening (I sing soprano in choir).

Finally I try calling a breast center I'd assumed was only for cancer patients. After hearing my tale of woe, the nurse who answers says, "Oh, you poor woman!" (the first caregiver to express any sympathetic understanding). The center director prescribes an androgen that magically eliminates the breast pain with few side effects except a little extra hair; my voice seemed to be naturally deepening to alto range anyway.

MENOPAUSE

Ah, the relief of menopause at age 53 after decades of period-related misery (hot flashes pale in comparison). However, about four months after stopping the androgen, my libido goes into steep decline. (I now understand how for women, as they age, sex can just go off the radar.)

In fearful confusion, a few months later I see my gynecologist, who offers an injection of testosterone. A week goes by—nothing. After three more days, I rejoice to experience anew that delightful spreading warmth. She prescribes testosterone in pill form.

A few months later, after presenting at a women urologists' career conference, during lunch I consult these specialists. They are unanimous that testosterone should not be taken orally as it may damage the liver. I should try a patch or a gel. The patch my gynecologist prescribes gives me hives. As she's retiring, she urges me to see an endocrinologist.

I'm reduced to begging an endocrinologist for a prescription. She refuses because "Testosterone is not approved for the treatment of hypoactive sexual desire disorder in women." I prostrate myself before her, crying, "Surely you realize there is no other treatment available to women? You don't care if this marks the end of my husband's and my sex life?!" She indeed doesn't seem to care in the slightest and sees me to the door.

I find my way to gynecology specialist James A. Simon, MD, one of the few physicians investigating low libido in women.[25] He explains that my brain and clitoris are now dependent on the testosterone that had effectively countered the estrogen in my breasts. He prescribes an easy-to-apply gel that works in minimal quantities. What a relief to discuss this with someone who understands and cares. He says, "Please tell your friends about our clinical studies." That I can't think of one woman I'm comfortable mentioning this to is damning evidence of the general silence surrounding

---

25 A most humane doctor's office: Intimmedicine.com

women's libido. Where is the grassroots support for this aspect of women's, and men's, health?

A HAPPY ONE

The above notwithstanding, my female body's story is generally a happy one. I'm grateful for all the ways my life has been easier than it was for my grandmothers—contraceptives, ibuprofen, tampons, microwaves, dishwashers, slacks, access to higher education, a choice of last name, leisure, search engines, and the chance at a healthy elderhood.

I've often enjoyed being a girl! There used to be nothing like the fun of new clothes and cute shoes. Now I can't remember the last time I wore a skirt or heels (I finally pitched a tangled mound of pantyhose). And coming full circle, I now much prefer undershirts.

At first it was hard to accept that my collagen had utterly given up. That I used to be able to get better looking doesn't bother me anymore—a profound and money-saving achievement for a woman. At this point, all I can do is put on earrings, apply eyeliner and lipstick, and smile. I try not to feel too bad about my upper lip—it was the smoking!

Who Lives Within This Skin?

Now I've lost my collagen
I don't care if I fit in.
I'm finally discovering
who lives within this skin—
    not in relationship
    to him or her or them

> or to what's past.
>> Beyond the stays of self-debates
>> let's see who is arising now with spine held straight—
>> who's firm of step upon a path she day by day creates.

I sing out, "Blessed art Thou, O Lord our God!" for the immeasurable body-enabled harmonies and comforts and joys my husband and I have been experiencing together for 57 years.

MUCH ABBREVIATED AUTOBIOGRAPHY OF A HEADACHE (HA)

Synopsis: Headache has been the bane of my existence for over thirty years. I have sought help from many physicians, including two neurologists, nine acupuncturists, three massage therapists, a psychoanalyst, dentist, endodontist, prosthodontist, reflexologist, yoga teachers, my sister, and my pastor.

PSYCH CONSULT APPOINTMENT 1 (MAY 2022)

JB: Starr, you remember I consulted you five years ago aiming to expand my self-awareness, since as a coach, my instrument is my consciousness. Among other benefits, you helped me extract value from my dream journal.

I contact you now way off kilter with pain. For over thirty years I've struggled with periodic bouts of intractable HA, but it's been daily since an infected tooth was extracted three months ago. I'm finally getting to talk to a neurologist next month. Now I also have a painful weakness in one leg that's impeding my gait—and here it is spring when I'm so eager to be out hiking; I see a PT next week.

What's tipped me into seeking this consult is my upcoming double implant surgery involving a sinus lift and bone graft (I can hardly believe I'm letting someone cut into those tissues after my experience with sinus surgery decades ago). With my history of dental trauma, I can tell I'm adding fear into this already challenging equation.

Starr: Tell me about your fear of dentists.

JB: Long story. My thumb addiction lasted until braces began the necessary reshaping of my upper palate—the first in a lifetime of dental interventions. Two left me with especially awful residuals. First my orthodontist fondled my breasts right before the extra thrill of tightening my braces to the max ("tight tighter tightest tightest tightest"), heightening the terror I experience both before and after these appointments. Second, during one of my countless root-canal-related procedures, a Novocaine needle damaged the nerve to my taste buds—evidently about a one-in-a-million occurrence. The dentist says that it takes six months for nerves to regenerate and that the damage probably isn't permanent. Meanwhile, my home-base feels foreign, dry and unsavory. Fear keeps me awake. Finally, after five and a half teeth-gnashing months, taste begins to return.

What I went through to quit smoking with no aids yet available is another example of the troublesome extent of my mouth-centeredness. My first attempt to give up cigarettes involved buying a pipe—my boss's idea, which he can hardly believe I take him up on. What a hilarious sight I must've been, a thirty-year-old short-skirted professional simultaneously knitting and smoking a pipe! I can't keep it lit, though, so I go back to cigarettes.

After getting sober, noticing that smoking involved the same hiding behaviors as my drinking did, over a period of months of praying for willingness to quit, I tapered off with the lowest nicotine cigarettes.

On my first day without, planned to coincide with a camping trip, I'm literally whimpering. A primitive part of my brain is conniving a way to smoke. On my first day back at work, my hands erupt with a rash that itches like mad. Within hours I'm ready to give up.

Uncharacteristically, I reached out to a new friend who has encouraged my dedication to this goal. He asks if I've ever experienced this rash before. Yes, at age twelve, when braces put an end to the comforts of my thumb. He observes that as I've taken away her thumb again, "little Janet" is kicking and screaming. He recommends reaching back to comfort and reassure her. Hugging a teddy bear might help too. My sweet niece, Leah Janet, gives me one of her teddy bears. To my amazement, this combination subdues the itch.

For months after, the craving nonetheless almost floors me. I obliterate pacifiers and so many carrots that my palms turn orange, impressing the children in my life. Sometimes my mouth feels empty enough to chew up chairs. At one point I give up and buy a pack of cigarettes; I smoke all of them, and they taste disgusting enough to finally cure me.

After my first big talk and then again after my first big consulting job, which I do not know how to prepare for or how to recover from, the relentlessly tormenting itch returns. I finally manage to see a dermatologist, who diagnoses herpes simplex—the virus that causes cold sores, of which I've had my share—and which erupted on my hands when I quit my thumb and then cigarettes.

Many years later, the week my first book is published, I happen to have a dentist appointment. He informs me that the prickling bumps on the roof of my mouth are a herpes simplex infection. As the book-related attention is welcome, this hideously painful new version of my typical stress response confuses the hell out of me. As with shingles, this virus can dig deep into nerves.

Now when my immune system is compromised or some primal anxiety is reignited, an infection may manifest in my upper palate. That's way more than enough, Starr. So in a nutshell, I'm anxious about the upcoming cutting into the roof of my mouth and how I'll manage that alongside my HA.

Starr: So a million neural pathways connect for you around your mouth—it is homebase. Your thumb, your built-in soldier, helped you survive childhood without worse psychosomatic problems.

While your mouth has given you a lot of trouble (as all crutches ultimately do), don't forget the pleasures it allows and how many worthwhile words you've generated.

Let's back up. Before we have access to language, our bodies store pain and fear that we're unable to manage or to soothe ourselves out of. Effective coping mechanisms, like your solacing thumb, limit the negative emotions stored. Any triggers related to what we have stored, though, will be embodied; that is, the body will somehow express it, like your herpes.

JB: Might hypnosis help?

Starr: Instead let's try what Jungian psychology calls "active imagination." For our next virtual appointment I'll guide you through this method, which engages imagery from earlier points in our psychic development to track the emotional root of our struggles. Resulting images provide a meeting point between our present-time consciousness and the painful emotions formed before we can talk, planting a light where healing may begin.

Over the Line

(for Kathryn Kaplan)
when did you learn to draw a line chalking
what you share from what's too dark to?

worlds may be colliding in your breast
yet your surface barely ripples

you have the right to remain unseen
but if you venture back over that line

you can become visible to yourself—
a perfect example of a human being

you lift your eyes
your unmanacled hopes wave in greeting from a hill

you climb and climb until you smile to see how far you've come
and when you lay your burden down
a sigh arises from your depths releasing lonely years
and what you've craved but dared not name lands in your lap
hands stop wringing
and get to work on the work that is truly your own.

APPOINTMENT 2

Starr: First I'll help you relax. Now I invite you to go back to when with no warning you are no longer the center of the world. You are alone in a crib in a different room, pulling your hair toward your mouth with your thumb-hand. Nod when you are there. Now you become Janet the mother going to comfort the hair-tugging Baby Janet.

JB: So as Mother Janet I'm standing at the door and soothingly explaining to the little one that she'll be fine; no need to pull out her beautiful hair.

[long pause]

Starr: Are you trying to teach her something that she's too young to understand? Yes? Then not being able to understand is compounding her shame about her displacement.

JB: Bingo. When Linda arrived, I falsely concluded not only that I'd lost Mom's love but that I caused this catastrophe. Holy cow.

Starr: Let's try again. This is a twenty-month-old baby.

JB: I am cuddling Little Janet, whispering "Sweetheart, you are first in my heart even when you can't see me. So now I'm cradling your little hand and kissing your hardworking thumb and placing it on your belly. Your hand likes this spot too; give it a pat."

Starr: Even as you're encouraging her to shift her focus, what she needs at this point are consolation and reassurances.

You can draw on your resourceful older self any time, befriend-ing yourself at different ages. You can comfort Little Janet, easing her adjustment to the loss of her soft curls and her secure place. To help heal any orthodontic residue, you can remove his hands and march out, confident in your soon-to-be-dazzling smile. You can function as the ally and friend of your previous selves whenever it would help, like right before your oral surgery. And at the onset of pain-associated panic, lengthening your exhales, you can move your attention to the Ground of All Being, our larger body, allowing yourself to be held.

Believing in your access to these supports will help break your habit of constantly holding yourself at attention. Consider how much weight you've been carrying your whole life. You can relax that strong will that's gotten you so far. A calmer self has been waiting to emerge.

JB: This all makes sense to me.

"As the body sheds its power, it would be lovely if each of us could shed the heavy weights that we carry for a lot of our lives."
—John O'Donohue

NEUROLOGIST APPOINTMENT 1

Following is the requested history I submit prior to my first appointment:

With no prior history, except for just-shoot-me hangovers, frequent head-aches commence at age 42 that I'm unable to link to any location, food, activity, or condition. After two years the headache settles in to daily. Pointless appoint-ments with three physicians lead me to a highly recommended neurologist who labels it "analgesic rebound syndrome" (I've been taking a lot of almost useless aspirin and ibuprofen and the Tylenol 4's not absorbed by cramps). He orders me off everything (I comply, although a shoulder injury is causing constant arm pain, which ibuprofen really was helping).

The jackhammering hell of an MRI reveals no clues, as I was certain it could not. He prescribes a tricyclic antidepressant, which reduces me to nervous-breakdown-level tears. Next is a calcium-channel blocker hard on my stomach and on my libido (he offhandedly laughs about the latter to his nurse). After a month, I see a New England Journal of Medicine article con-cluding that calcium-channel blockers aren't effective for HA. When I ask if he's seen the article, he says, "Well, that helped my partner's headache."

Finally I try acupuncture and experience the first relief in more than a year. Over the next thirty years, I work with many practitioners, each of whom has her own unexplained approach. Treatments vary unpredictably in effectiveness but usually help. When they don't or when no treatment is available, the headache sits for days like an anvil on my forehead, inducing wincing throbs. The best description I've found is "non-acute intractable HA."

Since an infected tooth was extracted five months ago, the HA has become daily. I'm looking at a double dental implant that won't be complete for another five months. Meantime I can't chew on that side. Unlike during previous bouts, repeated acupuncture has not helped at all.

Neurologist (sitting on a stool, so we're eye to eye): So it's been rough lately. I suffer from HA, so I understand. I'm guessing this new phase is TMJ-related. The temporomandibular joint or TMJ acts like a sliding hinge, connecting your jawbone to your skull. But since you won't be able to chew normally for several more months, we can't tell.

Here are samples of two of the newer migraine medications that are showing effectiveness with non-migraine-type HA. Have you found anything that helps?

JB: I usually get about four hours of relief from a low-dose THC edible without a loss of focus—although it's difficult to titrate the dose, given highly variable manufacturing and labeling practices.

When the throbs are regularly obliterating my concentration and I can't afford any fuzziness, I need Vicodin or something strong. While opiates and relaxants don't give me the normal amount of relief, they're better than nothing.

Neurologist: I'll write you a prescription for 15 "rescue" Vicodin.

JB: That's exactly how they work for me, but only for two or three hours. A prescription for medical marijuana would be helpful.

Neurologist: Our practice has decided not to seek a license to pre-scribe medical marijuana. Some of my patients are getting good results with Delta-8 gummies, a less psychoactive form of THC, which you can buy at the hemp store down the street. Make a follow-up appointment for a month from now.

NEUROLOGIST APPOINTMENT 2 (VIRTUAL)

JB: The first med, nothing. The second worked for the first week—I jumped for joy—but then it just stopped. Can you help me interpret how that might happen?

Neurologist: Let's try a once/month injectable that works as a preventative. Let me see if we can get the necessary insurance approvals—these drugs are very expensive. Come in next week and the nurse will teach you how to inject the drug. It may a take a month to tell if it's helpful.

NEUROLOGIST APPOINTMENT 3 (VIRTUAL)

JB: So three shots in three months and no change. So I need another 15 rescue Vicodin—that 15 has to cover 120 days of a daily condition.

Neurologist: Okay. Next is to get you approved for Botox. It should go through, since we can prove we've tried everything else. My scheduler will be in touch.

NEUROLOGIST APPOINTMENT 4

(This appointment is delayed two months due to paperwork screw-up.)

JB: I wrote a poem of hope about this Botox: "We make robots that outfox us, but a headache stays a big black box. Oh, please give me a cranial detox."

Neurologist: Hahaha. You'll just feel little pricks here on the base of your skull and around to the jaw. Botox may take a month to work.

NEUROLOGIST APPOINTMENT 5

Neurologist's Nurse Practitioner (NP): The doctor is sorry he can't see you today. So you've had these migraines for over thirty years now, and daily for the last two years?

JB (quaking with helpless frustration): They're not migraines. I don't understand why you use that term. And my noise sensitivity has really worsened. I can't go to restaurants or theaters.

NP: Let's go over your chart (there ensues a grueling and utterly disheartening review of every useless drug that's ever been prescribed for me).

NP: Let's try Topiramate, an anti-convulsant that's helped many migraine sufferers.

VIRTUAL NP APPOINTMENT (DECEMBER 2023)

JB: The dose of the anti-convulsant you said to work up to has made me as miserable as I've ever been in my life. I've been jumping out of my skin with agitation and being randomly attacked by weaknesses I conquered long ago, plus dry mouth extending all the way back to my tonsil scars, terrible loose bowels, and I can barely stand to look at food. And it's Christmas!

NP: Let's try Klonopin—it can help with anxiety. (It didn't.)

DENTIST APPOINTMENT

JB: How eagerly I've looked forward to your screwing in my implants. I am desperately hoping that once I can chew normally, this HA I've had every day since the extraction nine months ago will let go of my head. The neurologist thinks TMJ is a probable cause. What do you know about TMJ-related HA?

Dentist: Yes, it makes sense that you'll get relief once you're chewing normally again.

JB: Please take a close look at the roof of my mouth. See, I've been having another herpes infection—I need a Valtrex refill. How does it look to you?

Dentist: Here's something I hadn't noticed before. You have tori, a bony outgrowth along the ridge there. This is pretty rare and probably from clenching at night. We'll get you fitted for a nightguard.

(Note: I create a Nightguard Blessing Ceremony, praying to the Saints of Dental Appliances to further my mandibular health.)

CONVERSATION WITH MY SISTER

JB: Lin, do you have the bandwidth to listen to me wail over the phone a few minutes?

Linda: Absolutely, tell me how you are.

JB: You know how much I enjoy volunteering in the church kitchen twice a month. Well, last week I couldn't complete my shift because of the noise volume—I was crying as I biked home—I didn't have my earplugs because I've never needed them there.

And when I hosted book club last month and even at my crones' group, sounds I used to be able to tolerate now pierce my ears like shards. It's so awkward, I can't keep putting myself in these situations. I feel so fragile and touchy.

L: Janet, you're not fragile—you're the opposite.

Making Friends with Awkward

My guru whispers:
Why so worried and self-conscious?
What's to fret about faux pas?
Where's your chutzpah?
Touch some edges.
Toe some ledges.
Give effrontery a try.
Nudge an envelope or two.
Don't let awkwardness forestall you.
You're older:
Be bolder.

JB: Today I'm also a little sad about yesterday's touch-free "annual wellness exam" with my longtime internist. She cares not at all about my continuing HA, now that she's referred me to a neurologist. But I can't afford to get spun up over anything. I'm still discovering what self-care means. I've read that with chronic illness and pain, we need to allow ourselves to mourn what the illness is taking from us and to acknowledge that to be chronically ill can feel like living in a state of camouflaged grieving. Grief can be a sign of spiritual health. But until we mourn, we can't get to the bottom of the emotions we are feeling. And until we do that, we don't allow ourselves to be truly comforted. I am not done mourning.

L: What's helping you cope with the pain now besides the gummies?

JB: Knowing I have the love and support of so many. I feel yours. I've been asking more friends to pray for me. And I sing hymns on my bike, including "Come, Ye Disconsolate," and "Stricken, Smitten, and Afflicted."

L: What about "O Darkest Woe, Ye Tears Forth Flow"?

JB: Usually I come around to "What a Friend We Have in Jesus," and "Blessed Assurance," but I don't see "Brighten the Corner Where You Are" on the horizon. Thanks, Lin, you helped me over today's hump. On so many levels I cannot imagine my life without you in it—and all you have done and do for Mom, especially now since her stroke.

L: She's also my friend. Have you talked to your pastor?

> "If you have a fear of some pain or suffering, examine whether there is anything you can do about it. If you can, there is no need to worry about it. If you cannot, then there is also no need to worry."—Dalai Lama

CRANIOSACRAL THERAPIST APPOINTMENT

JB: I've been generally well—below the neck. But [synopsis]. The HA pain is manageable with gummies, but the hyperacusis—noise sensitivity—is really constricting me. I cower at noises that others perceive as normal. I've spread mats all over my kitchen counters to reduce the clinks of dishware. The only spaces I can relax in do not occur in dining and social situations. And so many people speak and laugh with a raised voice. So hyperacusis is a severely limiting disability, and there are many times when my ear defenders are inadequate or inappropriate.

LW: So you probably know this. The longer we have pain, the better our system gets at producing it. When pain embeds itself in nerves, like is true for you, nerves become extra sensitive, as if a leaf could set off a house alarm that then keeps firing off meaningless danger messages. When all these circuits are busy processing pain, you can't expect yourself to simultaneously be making decisions or coherently communicating. Pain also puts stress hormones into our bloodstream—causing more trouble in the short and long term.

Please lie on the table. [For the next half hour, her energy-directing abilities are opening little spaces deep inside my cranium.]

LW: Does your HA have a voice?

JB: It's the voice of fear.

LW: You've had a long time to make friends with that fear.

JB: Yes, now when fear arises, usually compassion for myself does too and acceptance of this condition as a natural part of my life at this point, rather than an imposition. Sometimes, though, the pain sucks me down a rabbit hole of neurotic fixation on itself, as if it's special and deserves a spotlight. Praying "Help!" boosts me out of that hole, as do the brave examples of my friends, although it's gotten really hard to know how to answer, "How are you?"

LW: As the mind stops trying to resolve what is unresolvable, we gradually become more comfortable with our limits and mysteries. You have an awesome body and constitution. Don't give in to despair, my dear. This is a bump in your long and amazing road, not the road.

(Note: My HA returns that evening, but her encouragement continues to buoy me.)

"When the shoe fits, we forget the foot."—Zen saying

PASTOR CONVERSATION

JB: I've been wanting to introduce myself. [We get acquainted.]

Pastor: So let me know more about this difficult HA.

JB: [synopsis] So I have two invisible physical disabilities that few people can imagine. We say in AA, "More will be revealed," and "This too shall pass." But at this point I can't be sure of either. As one treatment after another hasn't worked, to hope feels like I'm setting myself up. Do you know David Whyte's book, *Consolations*? He defines despair as a loss of horizon, a physical and psychological winter, which we endure until we find a new form of hope. I haven't found a new form of hope—nor have I learned anything useful about treatment after decades of appointments. Some days it's an hour-at-a-time endurance test.

Pastor: Thank you for opening up to me in this way. We all live with uncertainty, but when there's chronic pain, uncertainty feels like even more of an abyss. What fortitude it takes to keep from crumbling beneath repeated disappointments. It's a testament to your self-care and resilience.

JB: The worst is when self-pity creeps in. Tonglen reduces my isolation and self-pity. Do you know Tonglen? In this Buddhist meditation practice, as I inhale, I counterintuitively seek to connect with all others who are in pain. On the exhale, I send out an all-embracing compassion. When I remember this practice, my little world expands a little—like when we notice someone else's pain, some of ours falls away. My friends' prayers for my health also connect me to a Power greater than myself. Additional mercies arrive randomly.

Pastor: May we pray together; may I take your hands? "Great Physician and maker of Janet, lover of her soul, who's been with her from her beginning and will be at her end, surround her with your Presence before and behind, above and beneath her, that she may be assured of the constancy of your guidance and healing power. Grant her your peace."

JB: My tears are releasing both pent-up sadness and a present joy because, feeling so fully heard, I feel held.

PROSTHODONTIST APPOINTMENT (APRIL 2024)

JB: In his last-ditch attempt to help me, my neurologist sent me to you.

Prosthodontist (after exam and x-rays): The braces to correct your overbite pushed your jaw back in an unnatural way, creating constrictions where your jaw and ear connect. In the fetus these structures are fused and do not fully mature until adolescence, so early braces can cause problems like this down the line. Your tympanic plates at the entrance to your ear canal are also abnormally small, so it's understandable that you're sensitive to noise. Lack of support for your now arthritic jaw and all the dental work you've had have only increased trigeminal nerve inflammation and pressure on the ear canal. I will fit you with an orthotic device to be worn 24/7 over your bottom teeth. Every six weeks, I'll make adjustments to your bite and to the appliance, which will gradually pull your jaw forward, reducing the pressure that's been building for so long. With this small but critical movement, your HA and hyperacusis will ease. It's unfortunate that people only arrive at my door after years of suffering.

[June 2024: My encouraging prosthodontist reports that my jaw is moving well and that improvements will be gradual but not be steady; the HA has lessened a little, but the hyperacusis still limits me to quiet rooms where only one conversation is going on at a time.]

wish list

how I long to say
what a hard time
that was
what courage it took
what love.

WE'RE PUT HERE TO LOVE

CHAPTER 7

WRITING A SELF

"The great difficulty of writing is to make the language of the educated mind express our confused ideas, half feelings, half thoughts, where we are little more than bundles of instinctive tendencies."—Helen Keller

DISCOVERIES

In eleventh grade, writing a book report on Thornton Wilder's *The Bridge of San Luis Rey*, I arrive at what feels like an original response to a text. Without considering how unlikely my originality is, my mind leaps with joy to be working in this whole new way. Then in senior-year English, my poem in the vein of *Paradise Lost* garners my teacher's high praise. Faced with Housman's *A Shropshire Lad*, my boyfriend Bill hands in a spoof, expanding my awareness of possible responses to the literary canon. To express the feelings I'm starting to be able to articulate, I begin penning what feel like poems.

Once I start drinking, my poems and journals become increasingly black with *weltschmerz* and purple with narcissism.

WRITING EXPERIMENTS

Newly sober at thirty-three, I'm vibrating with restlessness in need of an outlet. Ideas for a book on medical education occasionally congeal, but I go no further than planning my outfit for the cover photo. I try writing a story: Tina (tiny, the way I feel) bikes into a magic realm and makes friends, with whom she faces dangers. This attempt to imagine an alternative reality teaches me that I'm meant to search for reality rather than invent one—I don't know myself well enough to be able to imagine anyone else into being.

I decide to submit something to AA's *Grapevine* newsletter. When I hit the carriage return on my ancient typewriter, I send the tall mug of tea in its path flying. I put the typewriter away.

"All writing is communication; creative writing is communication through revelation—it is the Self escaping into the open."—E. B. White

COMPUTERS!

As an endless reviser, I am losing the war with typewriters. Before word processors, there were no delete or save functions. Revising requires painting over errors with white-out fluid, fooling with minuscule pieces of correction tape, or starting the page over. Oh, how I envy the men with their personal secretaries ("Here, Mildred, retype this.")

Desktop computers arrive not a moment too soon for my productivity and sanity.

Virginia Woolf's *A Room of One's Own* offers another kind of support. She makes an airtight case for why writers require at least a bit of privacy and solitude. Even with a ream of feminist lit already under my belt, I had not arrived at this obvious point on my own. No wonder I often feel frustrated by interruptions. I start to get better at holding space for myself.

As I begin my coaching practice in 2002, I embark on a project I title "Mentor-in-a-Book." I seek counsel from an author with an agent. She instructs me on how to proceed, warning that without an agent, there's no hope of a book deal; i.e., where a publisher pays the publishing expenses, paying the author a percentage of any profits. I take all her advice about how to maximize my chances, but the only two agents who respond discourage me. I abandon this project.

WRITING LIFE

Then, about fifteen years later, an unexpected decline in clients frees up the creative energy that coaching, speaking, and designing programs have long been absorbing. I start a file called "Writing Life," into which I insert the questions and strivings at the heart of my being.

As I've previously discovered, the act of articulating an idea, hope, or goal followed by opening a file multiplies my receptors for ideas, people, books. Any free space on friends' thank-you cards that serve as bookmarks become packed with my scribbles.

I find with Thoreau that decayed literature makes the best soil. Organizing the composting riches of the passages that I've been culling for years further convinces me that I'm arriving at syntheses worth sharing.

Inside the House of My Head

My inner clearinghouse is open plan
and porous with porches and ceiling fans

Today's work and play and meals
bike ride, pain management, yoga, errands
generally self-organize
with wiggle room for when nothing cooperates—
systems freely multitracking.

Highly reliable inner clock reminds me as required—
best are hours when it's altogether off.

For reading and writing are comfy couches galore
with lamps and tables and tablets near windows.

Breezes keep ideas, phrases, hopes afloat
mingling and meandering.

       Silent conversations with my peoples
       arise like prayers
       and thread and weave, resolve or leave me—
       may produce a sigh or text or call or card
       or sometimes bread.

Bill's great photos—Skye, Stromness, Wales,
Newfoundland, Kauai—dot the walls
(he could hang one hundred more, and just as fine).

       Random melodies arise and fade—
       a mockingbird's surprising February repertoire
       breaks into Mozart's Mass in C
       and here's my husband's always welcome whistling—
       Siegfried, Little Rascals, Hendrix, Duke.

       Planning office keeps downsizing.

And for when shit will not be contained, a padded hallway where
I rant and pace.

Storeroom, full of:
Every bit of know-how
won from putting myself out there—
one trial and error after another
and revising and rerevising
in pursuit of semi-accurate expectations
of anything, anyone, myself included.
 Treasures of sweet memories
 (what no longer serves keeps deliquescing).
 Loose ends and yarn spilling from their bins
 and *yearnings in all shades of purple.*

 And here's a quiet chamber kept for Thee:
 O Christ, surround me.

Dreamcatcher's weathered every clime—
infusing Spirit, infinite, into this space and time.

STARTING A BOOK

I begin to hear myself say that I want to write a book, but I don't know where to start. For every project I've undertaken prior to this, a path to publication has been fairly clear and certain, without my paying anything for the privilege of consideration.

Stephen King's book *On Writing* urges prospective authors to build on what they have a keen interest in and some understanding of. So I start with what I've learned about adult development from my own journey from loneliness and alcoholism to meaningful relationships and professional success.

My academic writing habits work against me—lead with the most boring part (i.e., method), keep the focus narrow, embrace jargon, foot-note everything, and erase any hint of your heart or personality. The fight to escape the deadly orbit of these practices leaves me flailing. If only there were someone with whom I could discuss my project. But only one person in my extensive network has published a nonacademic book.

I need a writers' group. I ask the only member of my book club who belongs to one if I can join her group of four. I share labored-over pages with these readers, but I'm a long way from answering their questions about a target audience or a "comparable" book, and then the pandemic disbands us.

DRAFT #0 AND THE HAND OF DREAD

The next two years see many versions of Draft #0[26] under the general heading of "Human Becoming." For the most part, they are a dog's breakfast of observations, self-revelations, poems, quotes, and questions about everything that matters to me.

While my body is clearly responding—with insomnia, oral herpes, and nail-biting—my friends don't know how to respond to the unfo-cused pieces I share with them. I create a checklist to encourage any response (e.g., "no time," "subject doesn't interest me," etc.), but of course I never attach it. I feel like a bat unable to echolocate, alert to even the slightest returning information.

With author Michael Chabon, "The hand of dread returned many, many times to entwine its chill fingers among my inward organs." I'm grateful to novelist Elena Ferrante for commenting, "It is we who have

---

26 David Foster Wallace coined this perfect term.

authorized ourselves to be authors, and yet we resent others saying, 'This little thing you did doesn't interest me.'"

My mother, God bless her, keeps up her support, although reading some of my pain-laden passages must cost her (she suggests I get a cat). Brilliant cartoonist Roz Chast reported that her friends' response to her first work was, "I didn't know you were that unhappy." My mother and husband feel the same way.

Bill, however, also asks an obvious question: "Since ninety-nine percent of the people in your world know you as a high-functioning professional, why lead with the most difficult parts of your past?" Duh. I don't need to demonstrate *how* I acquired the skills I use in coaching; I can simply focus on the skills themselves—building on your strengths, arriving at a definition of success based on your values, communicating across differences, maintaining equanimity even when you feel devalued, increasing your objectivity, approaching conflicts as learning opportunities, navigating organizational politics, and building resilience.

While taking a walk on Christmas Eve, these sacrilegious lyrics come to me: "O holy night, my muse is brightly shining, it is the night of my new title's birth. Long lay the draft in sin and error pining, 'til this improvement appears and my soul finds some mirth. The thrill of hope, the weary writer rejoices, for yonder breaks the possibility of someday getting this book out of my brain and heart." Suddenly, I am able to craft a viable structure.

A PUBLISHING PARTNER FOR *EQUIP YOUR INNER COACH*

And so I make a real beginning, although I hit a wall whenever questions arise as to what I'll do once the writing is complete. Since I tried interesting an agent twenty years earlier, competition to publish has increased exponentially. This means self-publishing—a booming, complicated industry. Worrying aloud about this dilemma to a journalist friend, I gain an introduction to someone she knows who has just published a book with the help of a publishing partner—a category of professional I didn't know existed, who guides authors in bringing their book from concept to self-published product.

Knowing that Bethany Kelly, the partner I hire, will handle the dozens of angles that I know nothing about frees me up considerably. The first benefit of the contract I sign is a developmental edit enabling me to sharpen the whole thing up. Many more months of work see the completion of copyediting, cover and interior design, and all the rigmarole associated with sales that Bethany handles—like the dozens of steps required to set up an Amazon account (I'm glad to knit her a pair of slippers).

Bolstered by my closest colleagues' affirmations of its value, I'm proud of the final product—and relieved to feel satisfied with its utility. I do everything I can to publicize it, although I can't bear to ask friends to play the Amazon rating game.

Lines Tending Toward True North

i

Where I've scuffed and rambled
tripped over roots and brambles
lies a cleared path
only yards away.

ii

With my soul propped perpendicular

to the way things have been going
won't you sister me—
your beam lending strength to mine?

 iii

With the dogs of my ambition begging frequent walks
veering into driveways and dead ends
sniffing out new friends
I need a cat of quiet—
her peace and dignity
and welcome mystery.

 iv

When you've made another meal
of what you never want to taste again
try tearing your regrets and frets into tiny bits
and scattering them among the chickens.

 v

March is publishing her frisky winds again
stirring the ink in my veins
leafing through my pages
whisking aside what's gone dry
clearing some new ways to try.

 vi

Every loss
reveals what we are made of.
No darkness left inside
to be afraid of.

FACE-OFF

Janet 1: You ask why am I persevering with this memoir?

With visionary William Blake, I believe that "We are put on earth a little space / that we may learn to bear the beams of love." Writing this memoir has continuously revealed new glints and prisms in the beams I was put on earth to bear and to bear witness to. I am intent on doing justice to what God has given me. As Ecclesiastes exhorted, "Whatever thy hand findeth to do, do it with thy might."

Also propelling me are the hundreds of great authors' consciousnesses that have for decades been flowing through mine, lighting candles in my heart and mind, putting air in my tires. As poet Edward Hirsch said: "Most writers are readers who have spilled over."

Perhaps a bit of the "egotistical sublime"—a desire to lift up my own perceptiveness[27]—is also at play. After all this sculpting of my mountain of perceptions, this wish feels natural. It's not only writers who occasionally find themselves fascinating, though, and desirous of appreciation.

And I'm rich with access to creative energy, to spiritual nurture, and to the beauty of our great outdoors, as Part III hymns.

Janet 2: But *honey*, the fields of memoir and poetry are already way overplowed, and everybody's got stacks of unread books and many leisure-time options besides reading a book on actual paper. And the internet is awash in individuals talking about themselves. How will you reach more than a small circle of readers? You have to do all your own publicity, but your aversion to Amazon ratings and social media equates to no buzz, no "likes," and therefore minimal distribution.

Janet 1: But remember what our goddaughter Molly advised: Even if readers are few, my story and poetry will make a difference in lives in

---

27 Matthew Zapruder, *Why Poetry?* (Harper Collins, 2018).

ways I'll never know. How I've come to befriend myself may encourage others in this softening direction. Most women struggle with this self-acceptance, blaming themselves for their imperfections, even feeling conflicted about believing in their beauty and loving themselves.

> "An unconditional compassion for the human condition is the one true gift I believe a writer can give the world."—Femi Kayode

Janet 2: But how many will relate to you—off-the-charts self-challenging as you are? Plus, young people are coming up under such different conditions.

Janet 1: Isn't there something of the mythic here? In my underworlds I fought against confusing yet intimate foes and fears. Once I could face and name them, I worked free from my dark inner forces, equipping me to overcome collective attitudes that do not serve me. To stay true to my commitments to equity and service, I needed and received help in many forms. I have emerged with something of value to offer the community.

I never feel like a hero, though. I keep needing to *hit my own head with my own handmade wand,* as multitalented dramatist Anna Deavere Smith enjoined. Perhaps, also percussively, I'm just now hitting my stride as a creative writer. Though in the absence of an audience, it's hard to tell what constitutes hitting one's stride.

Janet 2: Self-anointing may leave bruises. Your intersection with current publishing conditions is not auspicious. And this evidence of thwarted ambition? You've stopped reading authors' acknowledgments because you're jealous of their magic-working agents. You don't go to author readings because your mirror neurons put you up on the stage being interviewed. You're preoccupied with how to distribute your memoir to friends. You want the impossible—to be both remarkable and comfortable. Plus, the Art is long and you are so old.

Janet 1: It's all true. And so is what trumpeter extraordinaire Miles Davis said: "Man, it takes a long time to sound like yourself." What's most important right now is that Mom wants to read this before she dies.

Her First Poetry Workshop

Child Janet to the poetry workshop came—
green, ardent, curious, and game.
She likes the virtual teacher right away—
wise face, kind voice, informal way—
small class, no showboatey turds.
Shared are passions to keep tangoing with words
and to find our special sauce and cabbage patch.
But how, she wants to ask, to build from scratch
a reading public, any audience
any sign that this is not a sad lost cause?
Yet doesn't an applause that's inner—
won from failures—
name another kind of winner?

HYPOTHETICAL INTERVIEW WITH AN EDITOR OF *POETS & WRITERS* MAGAZINE

P&W: How would you describe your memoir-writing process?

JB: Naturally I've read loads of memoirs. Many amaze and entertain me, but few encourage or inspire me. Of the how-to books, the multitalented writer Mary Karr's *The Art of Memoir* teaches me the most. She emphasizes that every inclusion must contribute to a narrative arc. I start most sections over.

I keep bumping up against the truth of brilliant memoirist Dani Shapiro's comparison of memoir-writing to making your bed while you're lying in it. When you're still evolving, what counts as an ending for your narrative arc?

I agree with author Philip Roth: "If you want to be reminded of your limitations every minute, be a writer—all the obligations are the more ferocious for being self-imposed." Right?

P&W: Yes, we can all relate to that.

> "Anything good takes time to ripen. When conditions come together, what has been latent in us for a long time may arise."—Matthew Fox

JB: My biggest challenge has been getting useful feedback. Without a guide or mentor or a diverse circle of writer friends, where do you start? Virtual courses and workshops are a beginning. But usually inexpressive faces—or worse, just names—can't really apprehend each other at the subtle levels required to ask sensitive questions, challenge assumptions, press for clarifications. Plus, even if you already know the person, before you can offer her useful feedback, you need some understanding of the writer's *goals,* which she herself may be unsure of, as we often are when we're attempting to communicate.

P&W: We all struggle to get—and to give—high-quality feedback.

JB: Both are interpersonally complex. Before I copped to the extent of these challenges, I didn't realize what I was asking of friends who must have been baffled by the documents I attached. I sweat these requests—I really had to screw up my courage. Would this friend be glad to be asked—or was she really hoping never to be asked again? Then, never fails—the minute I press "send," I notice a problem that begs to be fixed and am racked with sender's remorse, exacerbating the uncertainty I'm already feeling about my request.

P&W: Yes, sender's remorse seems to be a common experience—much worse if it's a final submission.

JB: The upside is that, even if you never hear back, you've discovered an important and fixable problem!

P&W: That's a healthy way to look at it.

JB: Then there's the matter of *taking feedback in,* which may occur months later—or never. To get the courage to expose my soft, naked belly to what may slice, before opening certain emails, I've had to give myself a pep talk.

"Revision is the chance for the writer's intuition to assert itself over and over," as author George Saunders points out. My instincts have needed guidance, and I've had to work hard to garner it—and ultimately have been glad to pay for it.

Spent / to Spend

When I consider how my life's been spent—
coffee brewed   onions chopped   points accrued
presents sent   stitches dropped
vacations craved   gloves lost   salads brought
paychecks saved   junk mail tossed

plans delayed   buttons pressed   milk bought

boots laced   notes addressed   dinners made

slippers knit   messes faced   mosquitos fought

deadlines hit   colds caught   trains boarded

toilets scrubbed   corners turned

zippers zipped   lessons learned   intros flubbed   lids unscrewed

candy hoarded   eggs flipped   nails chewed

I wonder how to live above this fray

free to find and pitch a bridge of words

that lands and plays in other minds

that tunnels into secret places

moves us closer to the spaces that we share

and to the love we must but cannot bear.

P&W: The poetry you've included adds an unusual dimension to your memoir. Which emerging poets impress you?

JB: I can't find entrance into most of what is called "poetry" in periodicals such as *The New Yorker*. One of my poetry teachers opines that *The New Yorker* is catering to academics who don't care how small their audience is.

P&W: You may want to expand your sampling of emerging poets.

JB: I agree. At the same time—have you read the fascinating *American Originality: Essays on Poetry* by recently deceased Louise Glück? This Nobel Prize winner praised poetry that "thwarts our urge to taxonomize," that "gives a long string to see what impressions may gather."

But if the images don't accumulate into a landing, what differentiates it from AI randomness? None of my dozens of well-read friends seek out poetry. One even warned against including the word "poem" in my book title. What is wrong with this picture? I aim to write poems that my friends may easily enter, but such poems don't seem to stand a chance of broader publication.

P&W: You draw an interesting contrast between two approaches—an imposition of order, as with rhyme, versus a goal of destabilizing order. Thanks for the Glück reference. A final issue you'd like to raise?

JB: Yes. The ratio of *wheat* (i.e., poetry that will last) to *chaff* out there is minuscule. As then editor of *Poetry* magazine, the great author Christian Wiman noted that this esteemed journal publishes only *three hundred poems* a year out of *over one hundred thousand submissions*. From *The New Yorker* article about Wiman, I also learn that whether this disproportion is a good thing or bad thing is, among the poet-elite, a controversial subject.[28]

P&W: I'll look into that article, thanks.

JB: Without an occasional dribble of recognition, how do you keep at it? But with all the distracting chaff, useful affirmation is hard to come by. Thousands of poets are submitting and resubmitting work with nothing to show for it but diminished morale and checkbook. Winning the poetry publishing lottery apparently depends more on the connections of your teachers and mentors—on what's trending, and on inscrutable literary gods—than on what's actually on the page.

P&W: A big subject we don't have time to explore today.

JB: One last question I'd like to raise: Most of us grew up saturated in male authors and artists. Don't you find that our literary—and in every other walk of life—*patrimony* is still interfering with women's finding their artistic voices? What does it take to fully awaken from our

---

28 Casey Cyp, "How the Poet Christian Wiman Keeps His Faith," *The New Yorker*, December 11, 2023, 20–26, https://www.newyorker.com/magazine/2023/12/11/a-poets-faith.

subconscious handcuffs and still-heavy leg-weights? On occasion, I've even wondered if there's too much "me" in my writing—I doubt any male authors ever wonder this.

P&W: This subject would make a great panel discussion. Thanks for your time. As you start submitting to journals and competing with your peers, I look forward to seeing some of your poems in print. Best of luck to you.

JB: I'll just close by saying that my mother thinks I've been a poet since I was a teenager. She says, "I hope someday your writing will be famous. That's how I feel about it."

Welcome, Muses

Who nudged a note into my inner clearinghouse
about how artists going way back have hooked up with you?

What's opening this door?
the pleading pressure of my vow to put fresh words around
the moving parts and mysteries of my soul—
words that spark to other hearts
that tune up cosmic cables
that find and rotate inner tires?

Ah, before I even start to coax and beg
three step into focus.
Quaking with audacity and need
I welcome thee.

Thanks for singing first, lyric Erato:

As you play with shaping janetland into melodic lines, fine-tuned designs

    share fun and victories

    be miserly with miseries.

Respect your own haphazard ways of catching universal threads

    of querying what's dim, of riding fired-up nerves

    of praising God—you've got the creds.

Welcome, strong Calliope, epic-queen:

As the author of your life

    keep conversing with your poet ancestors and sisters

    without envy or comparisons.

Their giant minds would root for you to find your own eccentric voice.

    Dig all teachers, random and pursued.

    Rely on your deep mine of content.

    Whatever has longevity will slowly render heat

    like a vein of coal in recompense for the attention paid.

Time and craft

    will separate wheat from chaff.

Thalia, muse of comedy:

trust gut

delete "but"

detail what's electrical

flashlight your quirks

tap what's audacious

be bodacious

so when the mockingbirds of doubt divebomb ambition's healthy

dogs

we'll calm your angst—

how about a smile and giving us some thanks?

Chorus:

If writing helps you feel the more alive, you're winning.

Bringing forth what is within you saves you. Believe it!

You can relax, but may your unrest be blessed.

WE'RE PUT HERE TO LOVE

PART III

ENERGY SOURCES

"Our fundamental relationship to everything larger than us—or our blindness to it—determine what kind of life is possible."—Mark Nepo

My energy sources—Creativity, God, and Nature—present as inseparable verbs, each releasing me from the bondage of self and each with Mystery at its core. With these hymns of recognition and praise, I press on the boundaries of the unsayable.

WE'RE PUT HERE TO LOVE

CHAPTER 8

CREATIVITY

"One of the lovely things a person can do for another person is to awaken the power and sacrament of their imagination."—John O'Donohue

BEYOND LUTHERAN SCHOOL

In ninth grade junior high school chorus, I thrived on a repertoire expanded beyond hymns. I auditioned for the Webster Groves High School chorus, only later learning that students from across-the-tracks Rock Hill were never selected. In Providence, getting to sing Brahms, Mozart, Stravinsky, Bartok, and Britten in the newly formed Providence Singers enormously deepened my appreciation for the musical arts. Along with later singing in Presbyterian choirs, these opportunities provided the most rewarding group experiences of my life. Making music together unites people, releases dopamine and oxytocin, and embeds sweet memories—while hopefully also giving pleasure to others.

Even after my mother's recent stroke at 98, and with her vision, stenosis, and arthritis issues, she can still accompany on the piano Linda's strong tenor and my alto on our favorite spirituals and hymns. This has been one of the greatest joys of our three lives.

My history proves that the early stoking of an imagination with literature, classical music, and visual arts is not necessary for acquiring a taste for art. The only decoration in Linda's and my childhood bedroom was a dingy gray needlepoint proclaiming "There rings a bell in my home so true that welcomes guests as nice as you." (I wanted it to say "rings a bell in my *hotel*.") Often my eyes longed for something new to throw themselves against. Rather than retarding my appetite for the visual arts, these longings seem to have whetted my appreciation for the riches that awaited me. The privilege of a liberal arts education and the good fortune of a partner with whom to enjoy art of all kinds more than made up for my humble start.

SHARING OUR CRAFT

Art begins in craft, in caring about detail, making the finest work we can, our particular version of what's good. This applies to excellence in all fields of endeavor—athletics, photography, singing, dancing, graphic design, ceramics, gardening, pies. There's great pleasure in sharing our crafts.

Not content with passive enrichment, artists turn nothing into something—nudging their craft into a creation that meets an unaddressed human need or throws fresh light on what's become familiar, nourishing others' imaginations.

> "Behind the storm of daily conflict and crisis, ... the poet, the artist, the musician, continues the quiet work of centuries, building bridges of experience between peoples, reminding [us] of the universality of our feelings and desires and despairs, and reminding [us] that the forces that unite are deeper than those that divide."—John F. Kennedy

WHAT PROPELS THE LEAP?

What propels the movement from being enriched by art to its active creation? Teachers who know how to both support and challenge a novice to aim high, and intense devotion to craft accelerate the motion.

But what starts the leap? And given patriarchy's continuing power, what helps a woman to believe in her creative capacity? We can't help but subconsciously absorb dehumanizing messages about the value of women. Before a woman can believe in her creative abilities enough to act as her own agent, she must detect and counter in herself these messages. People take us very much at our own reckoning. Nonconformity appears to be our only hope, as author Annie Dillard observed.

> "For only a relatively short time in the art world have women been giving a form of their own to what they have learned from life."—Elena Ferrante

Protective hesitation and taking a modest view of our abilities come much more naturally than self-confidence—a holdover from eons of grandmothers trained in silence and self-erasure and assured that pride goeth before a fall. I remind myself that there's no fall to fear and that I am rich with opportunities to be fed by as much art as I have time for.

> "We have been raised to fear the yes within ourselves, our deepest cravings."—Audre Lorde

NOT OPTIONAL

Art doesn't seem to be optional. The impulse to tell, paint, somehow convey glimpsed truths about the human condition, our fears and cravings, seems inborn. And as author John Berger noticed: "The talent to make art accompanies the need for that art; they arrive together."

And because human nature doesn't improve, we wouldn't expect art to. Today's art does not land with more primal force than those drawings of bison and stenciled hands in caves from eons ago. That our sexist, inequitable, overfed, undernourished, sedentary, sleep-deprived, violent culture is still producing art is evidence of our need for it and fuels my faith in humankind's, and art's, resilience. "If truth is that which lasts, then art has proved truer than any other human endeavor," as author Jeanette Winterson observed.

We're Put on Earth to Love

for Jeff

To tune in to a life form is to love it.
To love is to patiently await what's next.
Is there a name for seeking the woods no matter the weather—
and attending to every creature that presents—
female cardinal's subtle shading
redstart's velvet black and snappy orange
triumphant fern's unfolding—
each species worthy of our study
if we can but stand still
until whatever's restless, ill
dissipates into the Ground of all Being
begetting a serenity perfect for observing.

To praise with a camera is to reflect
a fraction of creation
back to the hurrying world so prone to forget that
we're put on earth to notice
and to love, to love.

PERSONAL RESPONSES

Each of us takes in the world via a unique combination of receptors. The "eye of the beholder" defines what we absorb. A wall of graffiti may appeal to me more than a painting worth millions. To discover the whimsy in a sculpture, I may need a child dancing around it. As often as I am aided by a critic's insight, I respond to art without knowing where the response originates.

I here gather words around a few of my most memorable responses:

* In Beethoven's *Fidelio,* my first live opera (1975, conducted by Sarah Caldwell—I've yet to hear another woman opera conductor), the chorus surrounds the audience while holding hands to sing the finale's triumphant hymn to freedom. I am delirious with joy (Jon Vickers and Christa Ludwig's recording still gets me dancing around and conducting the life out of my kitchen).

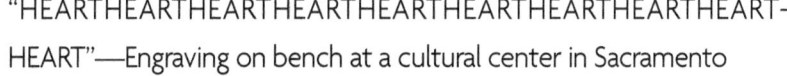

"HEARTHEARTHEARTHEARTHEARTHEARTHEARTHEART-HEART"—Engraving on bench at a cultural center in Sacramento

* Van Gogh's interpretations of stars, grass, trees, and human beings enter me like existence in love with itself—and sometimes simultaneously at war with itself. Nothing is muted. His self-portraits vibrate with an almost holy vulnerability, somehow sanctifying my own.

* In his late self-portraits, Rembrandt's eyes look across four centuries directly into mine. His eyes tell of strenuous wrestling with every human frailty and of the inextinguishable pleasures of being alive. Van Gogh said that Rembrandt must have died many times to portray what he painted.

* Though I'm sitting way back in the noisy free seats of an outdoor auditorium, Yo-Yo Ma's first bow across the cello strings finds, lifts, and floors me.

* The Met's production of Puccini's "Turandot" tingled every fiber of my being for four hours with melodies of ineffable sweetness and power, all elements unified in conveying earth-shattering longing, evasion, and finally fulfillment.

* Coltrane's "A Love Supreme," Pharoah Sanders' "The Creator Has a Master Plan," and much of Bach and the best sacred music sound as if they are being pulled from an endless Source, as if God's saying, "And there's plenty more where that came from!"

> "Between what I think and what you hear, there's this damned instrument."—John Coltrane

* Video artist Bill Viola's installation "Mary," at the altar of London's St. Paul's Cathedral, rivets me. The faces of the actors portraying Mary reveal every imaginable permutation of a mother's pride, wonderment, responsibilities, vulnerabilities, undying love, suffering, and sacrifice.[29]

* Actor Steve Buscemi's Donny (*The Big Lebowski*) perfectly captures the pull between trying to understand what's going on vs. giving up, with his ever-shifting facial muscles conveying the concerned bewilderment I often feel.

* Making my way around a floor at MOMA, I catch bits of enchanting harmonies. Finally I arrive in a gallery with forty small speakers at head height, placed in an oval, each broadcasting a voice singing Thomas Tallis' glorious mind-blowing motet *Spem in Alium* sung by eight five-voice choirs.[30] Standing in the center offers a perfect blend of the eight lines of harmony; standing next to an individual speaker, I hear one uniquely textured human voice.

---

29 https://www.stpauls.co.uk/martyrs-and-mary-by-bill-viola
30 In Teju Cole's new novel *Tremor*, I happen upon the name of this work of art: Janet Cardiff's "Forty Part Motet."

As each example reminds me of others, and knowing that all efforts at capture are doomed, I stop there. (You try summarizing your most meaningful interactions with art!)

"What was any art but [an effort] to ... imprison for a moment the ... life hurrying past us and running away, too strong to stop, too sweet to lose?"—Willa Cather

"Now there are a variety of gifts, but the same Spirit; and there are a variety of services, but the same Lord; and there are a variety of activities, but the same God who activates them in everyone. To each is given the manifestation of the Spirit for the common good."—1 Corinthians 12:4–6

A Glee Possesseth Me[31]

Decades of poems, notes and quotes
collect, co-mingle, cook, distill into
idea-blobs.
Some sprout cilia, scatter and collide.
Winners reach out limbs pulsing with truth.
Muscled phrases throb alive and flex.
Blood flows into paragraphs as they emerge.
A spine discovers itself.
Neurons connect.
A consciousness is born.
A heart arouses.

---

31 Phrase borrowed from Emily Dickinson.

Random bolts of light plus timely feedback
reveal what to excise, reshape, and rearrange.
Sure-handed sprucing up, massaging are but play.
So when she is delivered
stands up whole and sturdy
bundled in joy
feeling for the first time her oats
beginning her own journey and
conveying just what I've been striving to convey

I shout huzzah—
my inner writer's jumping up and down
we're doin' the neutron dance
brain effervesces
and for a minute I'm inebriate
and on my mountaintop may greet
    Dickinson or Woolf
    Mary Shelley, Oliver or Karr
    Annie Dillard, Patchett or Lamott.
A hand may reach within my grasp.
A mineral that once passed through a stellar mother
may bubble now in me fueling what's next.

CHAPTER 9

GOD

"Trust the universe. It is indeed a friendly place. Otherwise, you wouldn't be here right now questioning whether it is. Your very existence presupposes a benevolent force."—Lao Tzu

"Original Presence…"

Original Presence, Ground of all Being, Great Spirit, O Radiant Light—
that which is greater than all and present in each

Child awake in the middle of the night
spontaneously asks
without a goal or hope
    Who   am   I?
    A Cosmic Presence flash floods my whole being
    and washes me in   Awe
    and for a blink   I'm not alone   out here after all.

"We did not make ourselves. Who made us abides forever."—St. Augustine

BEYOND THE LUTHERAN CHURCH

Without any context for this solitary instant, when I awaken I am alone again.

After giving up on Mt. Calvary, I tried a nearby Quaker meetinghouse. A friendly silence welcomed me. I would open my Bible to Ecclesiastes, finding comfort in the lack of causality between human actions and outcomes. ("The race is not to the swift, nor the battle to the strong … for time and chance happeneth to them all.") Once an elderly woman took my hand after a service and smiled into my eyes with eyes that shone with a light I've never seen. The radiance of her face transfixed me—as if she were seeing in me a light of which I'd been unaware.

Ten years of daily drinking nearly extinguished any trace of it.

Once I'm finally on my knees in shreds, what felt exactly like the Hand of God lifted the ton of bricks that was my drinking off my back, and resurrected at age thirty-three, my life began.

"You don't have a soul. You are a soul. You have a body."—C. S. Lewis

THEOLOGICAL CURIOSITY

Meister Eckhart taught, "It is a lie, any talk of God that does not comfort you." While it didn't offer any comfort or much useful information, my Lutheran education did beget in me a lifelong theological curiosity. And as my alcoholism left behind a God-shaped vacuum, I arrived at AA ready for step eleven: "Sought through prayer and meditation to improve our conscious contact with God." I availed myself of any help in furthering this conscious contact.

At first I could barely sit still enough to pray. I started small: "God, thank you for my sobriety and my consciousness and my little faith that is growing." An AA friend gave me a die with "GOD" on all six faces and recommended that I paste this sign on the back of my office door: "Dear Janet: I know what I am doing. Love, God."

"The only thing that concerns God is your faithful use of your freedom. ... The whole question is whether you have used the things which are given to you in order to learn how to love. ... God does not ask for the psychologically impossible, ... for anything unattainable by me."—Father Teilhard de Chardin

SPIRITUAL SEMINARS

As if custom-made for me, a woman in my home group hosts spiritual seminars in her home. A Buddhist priest teaches us to chant *Om Namah Shivaya*—one meaning of which is "I honor my own inner divinity." That I have any divine light inside me arrived as such good news! And a Catholic priest likens God's love to radio waves that never cease broadcasting. Even if we feel like we're only tuned in to our own miserable frequency, our inborn receptors are scanning for a higher frequency signal. There are an infinite number of channels to the Divine.

But a strong habit of self-reliance often generates an interfering static. We tend to overdo our autonomy, that strength that's helped us survive. But this assumed independence limits our ability to pick up signals offering possible aid and guidance.

take and receive

bathe in greens, tender greens, softly shimmering greens
catch the hymn-spill of streams
    playing down over boulders and moss-splendid trees
bow to jack's pulpit, ginger, violets, and bluets

sup on pure milky petals of trillium
    dance with ferns down steep hillsides, unfurling, cartwheeling
may thrushes' arpeggios rinse you of sin
as you kneel to receive every blessing
    every kindness of spring.

CHURCH

Desiring to expand my circle beyond newly sober alcoholics and to participate in the sacred music that gladdens me and in the social missions central to Christianity, I begin attending a Presbyterian church.

Building a church community takes a few years of regularly showing up; volunteering for any service role speeds things up. Lasting friendships that I've made this way are a boon.

> "God is the universe's consciousness. The more we wake to holiness, the more of it we give birth to, the more we introduce, ... the more God is 'on the field.'"—Annie Dillard

But it is the opportunity to worship that draws me. To change the mind of humans about God, Jesus came. The unbounded, historically unprecedented love of Jesus for humankind eases my acceptance of my own and others' weaknesses and contradictions. Jesus' cross teaches me about the redemption possible when self-importance dies and how the whole horizontal span of human breakage may be healed by the vertical flow of Grace. And singing and praying in a welcoming sanctuary join me to other seekers and to the good that is in each of us. When I am fully present, especially during Holy Communion, my heart swells with gratitude for the gifts of the Spirit and for the lived faith of my ancestors that I am privileged to inherit. How firm a foundation!

As with AA, during church I take what I can use and, patiently and usually successfully, disregard the rest.

"The kingdom of heaven is within you."—Jesus

RECEPTORS FOR THE DIVINE

Only gradually have my receptors for what's holy and for the Love that has always been mine multiplied. When a Korean children's choir ran to embrace everyone in the church, singing "Jesus Loves Me," my heart overflowed my eyes. As a child, this song was empty syllables.

Within my quieter and more spacious heart, live sacred music begets upwellings of sweet-tasting tears. It is as if familiar hymns have been accumulating impact in a storage bin in my soul. These sentences represent me here about as vividly as a match does the warmth of a blaze.

"Silence is a harmony more beautiful than any other harmony."— Anthony de Mello

MY PATHLESS PATH

Inner stillness—when God feels nearest—I know to be both a gift and an achievement. Even when I've protected time for solitude with the intent of staying fully present moment by moment, random ideas about relational responsibilities and other obligations interfere.

A few weeklong silent retreats/advances have substantially boosted my ability to make use of shorter intervals.[32] In order to sense the unlimited friendliness of my inner teacher, early on I needed a week of silence and of forgoing reading to identify the voices my mind had been hosting that were not mine. The clarity of my awareness finally pierced the artificial authority of my superegoist vestiges. "Poof!" Intervals of a peace beyond the struggle to understand anything are now possible.

UNASKED, ANSWERED PRAYERS

Has something splendid you wouldn't dare to even wish for ever landed in your lap? The first unasked, answered prayer I noticed followed a friend's expression of love arriving on a day when I badly needed one, then like a cherry on the top, a rainbow!

On a larger scale, it could only be with help from a Power greater than myself that, instead of decaying into delusions, my wounds have been healed and transformed into compassion for myself and others.

Divine help with forgiveness has also arrived. Discovering that I'd be spending a holiday with someone whose presence I could not welcome, I crumpled in despair. Within minutes I was praying for rescue and swiftly received forgiveness for my hardness of heart, freeing me to focus on what we share instead of on all I can't make sense of about her. Mercifully overriding my entertaining sense of superiority, God greatly reduced my self-induced suffering in this situation.

Even just "help" or "thanks" momentarily softens me, pauses my self-reliance, and dips me toward the Light. Victory to that Light!

---

32 Dayspring in Gaithersburg, MD, with its rolling acres of pilgrim-trod paths, is my go-to silent retreat center. Please see pp.132–133, on "giving yourself restorative breaks" in my book *Equip Your Inner Coach: Personal, Career, and Leadership Development in an Uncertain Age* (2022).

ENERGETIC FIELD

Praying for someone, bringing into my consciousness my care for them, activates a subtle energetic field and also opens me to receive their prayers. Following my father's passing, my friends' prayers steadied me through this ordeal. During the time I was suffering from complications from pandemic-delayed sciatica surgery, friends' and loved ones' prayers kept me out of despair—as they have during my hard months of headache.

Some people pray by actually connecting with those in need, offering help, bringing homemade chicken soup. The slippers I knit feel like connective prayers; when recipients wear them, they may feel a boost of my care for them and my hopes for their comfort.

MY GO-TO PRAYERS

Prayers that have been offered over centuries carry extra power, like the Lord's Prayer does for many. These are the ones I most often turn to:

Metta (ancient Buddhist lovingkindness meditation)
May my/your mind be clear.
May my/your heart be open.
May I/you be filled with lovingkindness.
May I/you be healed.
May I/you be a source of healing.

From St. Teresa de Avila
Her heart is full of joy with love, for in the Lord her mind is stilled.
She renounces selfish attachments and draws abiding joy and strength from the One within.
She lives not for herself alone, but for the Lord of Love in all.
and swims across the sea of life, breasting each rough wave joyfully.

Let nothing upset you, let nothing frighten you.

Everything is changing; God alone is changeless.

Patience attains the goal.

Who has God lacks nothing. God alone fills every need.

FROM THICH NHAT HANH

* At meals: "When we eat bread, if the Holy Spirit is there, we can touch the whole cosmos deeply, as the bread contains the sunshine, a cloud, minerals, time, space."

* A mindful walking meditation: "I am safe. I am home. I am at peace. I am free. I am here. I am now."

* "Hello, my restlessness. We will be okay."

Fed by Shenandoah Autumn

jutting cliffs pared down from plates colliding half a billion years ago
   I hike beneath
      rejoicing that to them
         I'm less than lichen, matter as much as this trickle of rain
more nerve cells branch in me than in these beeches, oaks, witch hazels, ferns—
      but they recycle every fall
      while my decline is long and linear
cushioned by the service of each leaf, feet greet this trail—
      nose savors bouquet
         of a million fertile deaths
woods beckon like a chapel, yellow-lit

---

tendering to the wind
    their used-up food
      to shower me in gold
evanescent are these sacraments whereof I here partake—
    feeding for a minute hungers
        far too deep to name

CHAPTER 10

NATURE

"We are each like a well that has its source in a common underground stream which supplies all. The deeper down I go, the closer I come to the source which puts me in contact with all other life."—John Welch

OUT OF DOORS

Only out of doors did my father fully relax. Every childhood vacation was spent camping on a sweet spot on a Missouri river where he could fish, spots that we had utterly to ourselves for days. No parking lots or outhouses or river rafters. Happy times.

So it was a boon for our family when he purchased a hundred-acre property two hours southwest of St. Louis, with hills, woods, ponds, an abandoned mining pit we could dive into, a stream, and an upper field for growing hay for beef cattle. His planning, engineering, construction, land and water management, and vehicle- and machine-fixing skills, with Brian's and Mom's help, enabled him to create what we lovingly called the "farm." His three kids, their spouses, and his five grandkids explored this land in all seasons.

Together, we all enjoyed Mom's delicious meals and playing the card game "Oh Hell" after dark. Group and individual activities included fishing (of course); swimming (naked whenever possible); bird-watching; discovering wildflowers and flying squirrels; hiking country roads; partaking of the holiness and fun of snow; stargazing on mattresses with cats, exclaiming at any shooting star; whirling and dancing beneath lightning; and sledding our brains out under ideal conditions.

Eben Shantz; Fred, Andy, and Libby Wetzel; Leah Janet Shantz

Me having a ball.

It's never too late to have a happy childhood!

My August Day

Strip and ease
into our oak-surrounded pond.
Cows snort and low nearby.
Hawks circle screeching.
Cicadas peak and decrescendo—
my kind of summer jazz.

Crunch down gravel road in fleeting company
of dragonflies and monarchs crows, cardinals and buntings.
I smile at hardy Queen Anne's lace, orange trumpet vine, and horsemint.

Bend with Mom to gather string beans, okra, and tomatoes—
laugh at stalking cat and try to at our cranky knees.

Silently commune with Dad upon his deck
with views of land that's his and sky that's God's.
Purple martins fish the air.
Cuckoos kowlp-kowlp-kowlp from cedar grove.
Red summer tananger and mate in sunny yellow
drop by like guests to bathe.

I take in with every sense and pore—
no loss can rob this savor
even if I never get to
pass this way again.

Each of us treasures particular memories. Mine include absorbing the peace of cows while singing to them (ours preferred "Lida Rose" to "Gary, Indiana"); picking thorny blackberries at their sweet peak, purple juice mingling with our sweat and blood; wandering to my heart's content in winter woods such that shuffling through dry leaves still sounds to me of freedom; tramping in heavy snow on our farm road guided along by trunks of familiar trees, feeling as if I have the world to myself.

Country Kirke

Keen to scatter hay and breathe with animals
I zipper up against March wind to help Dad feed the cows
while Mom perfects blackberry pie and sets her hair for church
where we're expected to confess
that we are sinful and unclean, eternal punishment deserving.
Lenten hymns with harmony by Bach redeem the hour—
my alto line familiar as Mom's melody.
We settle in for deadly sermon—
Mom and I press shoulders and hold hands.
In his corner Dad breathes heavily—
is he here or circling old sins or new?

Released back under heavenly blue
I locate God in cirrus tails and swirls
and in my mother's laugh
and in the fine long lashes of a calf.

DAD'S END

Meanwhile, the damage caused by Dad's drinking steadily escalated from the late 1960s. In all his moods, Orville Wetzel ruled with a commanding voice and a powerful physical presence. While never touching us in anger, Dad's alcohol-fueled words scarred each of us, especially my brother. The next morning, he never gave any sign of remorse; maybe his blackouts were that total.

Understanding that his paranoia, barbed irrationality and, finally, his cruelly botched suicide were not reflections of his true self scarcely reduced our pain, my anger. His death in 2008 finally freed Mom to start her life afresh; she's done a splendid job.

Gradually, gradually my empathy for him, for me, for us replaced the bitterness. The positives of what he gave to us, his careful stewardship and care for us over his best years, came to outweigh the disaster and burden that alcoholism condemned him to become. As a father, he gave us hundreds of times more than his father gave him. I'm afraid that Dad never believed himself to be worthy of love, and the drinking confirmed it.

FULL CIRCLE

Yet nothing could've prepared me for his posthumous gifts. Several years after Dad's death, I arrived at a retreat center where all of the trails have been reverently walked by pilgrims over decades. As I descended on the first trail, my father's spirit flew into my heart space as if he had been waiting for this opportunity to fully reveal his love. This transcendent gift still staggers me.

Then a few months after that retreat, on a pilgrimage path in Japan, I was alone with our guide, whose father died the same year as mine. On a section of the trail sacred to those wishing to commune with their ancestors, she tilted her face to the sky and waved with both palms up, saying, "Hello father, hello father," and I wave up too, saying, "Hello father, hello father." A full circle of energy connected as Dad and I welcomed each other home. Our fathers who art in heaven…

Now sometimes when I am alone in the woods, he's company. Intertwined, Dad and I are joined not only by an alcoholic gene but also by a nonstop pull to be outside.

Plot

Even more ineffable and definite than a need to fish
can be a pull to tend
one's own dear plot of earth.
Bred into me as if a green-marked gene—
my father's legacy
along with craving drink
we need a bit of land.
A yard with woods is now within my keep
and worth the wait
and ripe with work—
palms peel
are proud with callus.
Wrestling with untended years of vines and weeds
I start a path.
I will care for land and trees
and they for me.

LEARNING TO NOTICE BIRDS

I emerged into adulthood recognizing only the most common birds. Our brains don't register a sound until it rises above competing noises in our heads and surroundings. Birders we meet at parks help us to put names to the calls we're beginning to notice. With practice, we get better at using binoculars.

Just as their decline accelerates in the mid-1980s, we fall in love with songbirds, especially the wood warblers. Bill installs a pump-powered stream facing our back door to offer a drink and bath to these precious beings on their long flights north to breed and south to winter. We take advantage of every second to admire them. Nothing nails me to the present like a warbler. Poet Kay Ryan called such thrilling arrests a "paradoxical vacation of perfect attention."

One of the most elusive qualities of birds is their unpredictability—a bird may appear out of nowhere and withdraw in an instant. But because of the wren house Dad made, we are treated to the house wren's exuberantly liquid pour for many spring and summer days. I tend to get emotionally involved in the nesting drama that has unfolded a bit differently in each of the last twenty-five years. Pointless new questions are always emerging: Does my nearby presence on the patio register at all? Do they sleep right next to each other? Encouraging its chicks to fledge, is the parent aided by any memory of what it took to fling itself out of the known world into the bright unknown? Just as with my study of human beings, the longer I observe birds, the more perplexing and fascinating are the differences I notice.

For an unprecedented couple of weeks this spring, arriving like a blessing, a wood thrush fluted nearby a few times a day. Thrush music, more than any other, rinses my ears of motor-residues. Windows closed, most people miss out on natural gifts like this, and with a clear conscience, many contribute to the decline of threatened species by having their lawns treated with innocently named products (TruGreen, NuLeaf) that are killing insects on which birds depend, as well as pollinators on which our food supplies depend. Apparently the ecology courses their children take don't cover what's going on in their own backyards, which they rarely use but which they pay to have trimmed to leaf-free perfection by three high-powered machines once a week, even in droughts when the grass isn't growing. I have to restrain myself from additional ranting here.

> "Old rocks remind us that the earth has been beautiful from the beginning."—Catherine Raven

GARDENING ON OUR ONE-THIRD OF AN ACRE

Starting me off in my other area of passion, when I was little, no other adult shared with me her enjoyment of anything the way Granma Wetzel did her garden. Shortly before her death, she gave me an asparagus fern to take to Rhode Island; it stayed with us for decades. Bill's Aunt Maxine, our only East Coast connection, added to our indoor plant collection and taught us how, even in winter, plants reward examination.

When Bill and I began improving our one-third of a partially wooded acre in Falls Church, Virginia, Bill's mother, Gerry, provided essential help.[33] She served as a Master Gardener at the renowned Missouri Botanical Garden and brought an elegant sense of design and beauty to every single visual decision (fortunately, a talent her son inherited). Gerry encouraged us to transplant trillium, bloodroot, bellflowers, and more from her deep backyard.

---

33 Blessed with many forms of intelligence, Geraldine Russel Bickel (1920–2013) could've directed her energies in many directions but didn't, because her good husband really preferred that she not work. But in every community college art course she took, she showed promise. With Gerry's great taste and instinct for bargains and my distaste for shopping, what a boon to happen to be the same size as Gerry, as she would often soon give me her bargains.

I continue to trade plants with friends and dig bulbs from properties about to be bulldozed. We have planted about 135 species of flowers and shrubs and many species of trees (not including a number of failures, naturally), adding to the existing tulip poplars, oaks, maples, wild cherries, and hollies. I have a different relationship with each plant; most feel like friends. Thanks to Bill's strong back and eye and by following our love of beauty, we have created a from-every-angle lovely botanic garden.

ADDICTED

Our property backs onto a road that now carries four times more speeding traffic than it did when we moved here in 1995. Plus dozens of heavy trucks bang, banging, barreling by a day. Worse, we sit in a large shallow depression such that every one of the echoing construction projects and lawn crews within a couple of blocks in all directions are visited upon us. Moreover, way beyond statistical probability, my presence anywhere attracts leaf blowers.[34] High-class problems, I know.

Beyond a genetic basis for my dying to be outside, I discover physiological excuses. Homo sapiens co-evolved with symbiotic bacteria present in the soil; nearness to the microbes in humus boosts serotonin levels. Intimacy with Mother Earth also stimulates production of oxytocin, a bonding hormone; turning my achievement of a compost pile and worm farm, I inhale a gloriously complex fragrance. Moreover, the repetitive patterns, like leaves, gaps in tree canopies, and ferns put us at ease.

Plus, there's the consoling company of my lilies, lobelia, coleus, geraniums, euphorbia, and caladium, and the chance to share a moment in space/time with an increasingly rare bird, butterfly, dragonfly, or bee.

---

34 I'm ready to fight back. Any reader with any ideas about how to organize against leaf blowers, please contact me at janetwbickel49@gmail.com

So naturally I'm obsessed with looking out, with windows, preferably wide-open. I can't completely relax in windowless rooms, and if there is a window, I need to be facing it. My family also humors my going around turning off overhead lights. On planes my twitchiness triples without a view of the earth or sky. Often I'm the only person looking out the window at all this free scenery! So, ironically, if there is a window seat on a plane that you can't actually see out of, that'll be the one I draw.

Rereading Mary Oliver

I have been reading Mary Oliver again—
her creed and mine agree:
   go outside
   slow down
   humbly notice what is stirring
   what's enduring.

God keeps me in riches—
redbuds, dogwoods, cherry blossoms
give way to iris, rhododendrons, lettuce
then come corn and peaches to bite into—
all the plenties of high summer feet caressed by sand and grass—
then crickets' company consoles me as nights chill
and maples flame up, gingkoes glow and melt my heart
and woods brew up perfumes of leaf decay
and ease me into afghaned hours gazing
at the intersecting wristbones of my pals, our trees.

And then I am delivered
    into another spring—sap rising everywhere.
A robin trills an extra lilt into his sentences
    then zooms off after she—
    they flutter-leap and dance up breast to breast
    till a rival breaks that tango up
    and female takes to lightly preening as if innocent.
Lady towhee sports a suit as nifty as her fellow's
    and even sings as many tunes and
    shows up at the one spot on the stream where she will bathe.
    If it is occupied, she waits, then takes her own sweet time.
Entering my patch of woods
    hushes my immediate frets.
    I pat encouragement onto these sisters' skin
    and they nurture, calm, delight me.
    I can't give them anything but love.

But, Mary, can you teach me
    how to stop gnashing my teeth—
    as one motor after another after another
    assaults my ears and soul
    and how to keep my heart from tearing
    as yet another big tree disappears?

Her spirit walks nearby and sighs:
    Ah, the trade-offs of conveniences.
    Yes, we mourn what's lost

and so we welcome every bee and
peewee's wood pipe echoing
lily-of-the-valley's heaven scent
dawn's lesson in group singing
wind chimes mixing cheer with air
a bunch of rosy radishes to share.
Let the daily news from trees and sky
seep in deep
and ever deeper.

ABUNDANCE

Nature has never fed me more bountifully than on a night hike in a rain forest in Costa Rica. Our guide flashlights dozens of frogs, spiders, bats, a line of leaf-cutter ants, sleeping birds (a completely motionless bird!). The dark thrums with subtle vibrations. Uncountable species have been thriving together here for eons, of which the coarse net of my senses detects but a fraction. This overawing surroundscape both affirms and redeems my insignificance. Until this hour, "biodiversity" was just a word.

Within my wide biking circumference, in every season I pay homage to dozens of resplendent mature trees and also in spring to favorite forsythias, lilacs, and azaleas. My appreciative attachment to these beings makes me vulnerable to their loss.

In groves growing from one root, aspen trees are sisters. When I am among them, they sister me—the wide-open eyes on their bark beckon me, their leaves sing and shimmer. Last summer, hiking in one of the country's largest contiguous aspen forests, I was unprepared for the hundreds of aspens scarred by fools' initials; the sight destroyed me. Many who believe they love Nature are in fact defiling her.

> "We forget that nature itself is one vast miracle transcending the reality of night and nothingness ... that each one of us in his personal life repeats that miracle."—Loren Eiseley

TETHERING

I require tethers. Witnessing the sun's lip tipping above or sinking below the horizon steadies me and my yoga tree pose; I know exactly where I am in relation to our Father Sun and to the blessing of the coming day or night. And tracking our lunar scamp links me to millions who've gazed at her with hearts cratered with hope, wonder, terror. When it's not too cold, I greet my winter boyfriend, strong-striding Orion. When the mosquitos aren't too awful, my hammock rocks and treats me to the geometries of the millions of hands of chlorophyll above me that absorb enough energy from light to make a world.

WE'RE PUT HERE TO LOVE

BEFRIENDING

"There is no knowledge so hard to acquire as the knowledge of how to live this life well."—Montaigne

BECOMING VISIBLE TO MYSELF

Self-study at age 75:

* Innate are my extraverted energy and my don't-fence-me-in need for autonomy and for action. What feels like inertia to me may to others resemble ADHD.

* Assuming that I had to earn my place in the affections of others amplified my self-challenging achievement drive. The wastage of my drinking decade spurred me into overdrive as I attempted to make up for lost time and the betrayal of my gifts.

* My upbringing instilled in me extremely useful senses of organization, responsibility, punctuality, and thrift, which I struggle not to overdo, as we all must with our strengths and values.

* My self- and world-investigative drives are hungers fueled in part by a need to avoid boredom. I counter my tendency to focus on what's next by savoring what's nourishing in the *present*. These hungers feel kind of divine—God-shaped holes.

* The fruitfully unpleasant work of learning from my negative emotions was greatly facilitated by superb mental health practitioners. With

help, including from my dreams, I learned to work with the information contained therein and to help others to do so.

* Lacking peers or identification with any group outside of AA necessitated a self-reliance that continues to interfere with my accepting instruction.

* My early loneliness shaped in me an intense appreciation of old and new friends—my superpower of multiple, non-intersecting circles: My and Bill's birth families; my gloriously extended and varied AA family; longtime professional colleagues scattered all over the country; friends from the three churches in which I've been slightly active; and friends from Bill's graphic design career. In high-quality relationships, we discover lovely affinities among each other's eccentricities and how to support each other through our losses, impairments, and insecurities. The love we give comes back around, often in ways we could not have imagined. In collaboration with others, we become visible to ourselves and more of the world becomes visible to us.[35]

beating the weary dismals

tears want to form but cannot start
sobs catch near the surface

you put your pants on backwards
even your pots and pans look down on you

---

35 I owe this phrase to the memoir of a friend, Dr. Kathryn Kaplan: *Becoming Visible to Myself: An Unexpected Memoir* (Christmas Lake Press, 2023).

your angers and regrets gang up against you
as if they'd never been released
so the news and weather don't much matter
nor does a healthy lunch

something big is turning
into something else
with persistent undertows of loss—
more lessons, never sought, in groundlessness
and your problems start to seem somehow ridiculous

so will you, friend, remind me again
how when in us a joy is born
of soul or scent or tongue
of eye or ear or skin
we inhale it slowly in
a moment of bliss, pay attention to this—
this is how we win.

"Wouldn't take nothin' for my journey now."—Spiritual

HITTING MY STRIDE IN LOOSER GARMENTS

Becoming fat with friendliness toward myself has taken my whole life.

During phase one of the self-improvement project that staying sober seemed to require, my inner critic overdid it. I listed the need for others' approval, followed by resentments for not getting it; belief in both my superiority and unique defectiveness; fear of being left out; anger at being

169

misunderstood; exaggeration of my frustrations and peeves; perfectionism; absence of self-discipline; self-centeredness; wasting time on attempts to guess what people think of me; and undervaluing my own progress!

Here are examples of my progress in letting go of the notion of progress:

* Less than/more than symbols (< >) filled my journals—as in "It hurt > than last time." Once I realized that these comparisons never produced insights, I gradually eliminated this chronic assessing and measuring of myself.

* Rather than engaging in mortal combat with tasks requiring website, mechanical, or technical skills, I get help asap. At first I only pretended to laugh at my incompetence—now my chuckles are more audible and sympathetic.

* The trance of scarcity I naturally acquired during childhood I've gained substantial release from.[36] Instead of habitual assumptions of insufficiency, I have faith in my access to everything I need.

This internal softening enables me to notice other constrictions—such as all-or-nothing dualisms. More accurate is both/and—both faith and doubt, your truth and my truth: "I love you," and "I need time alone."

All this easing up has boosted access to my imagination and sense of humor, enabling a more graceful handling of each day's impediments. When I detect that I'm unnecessarily holding myself at attention (to assure, for example, that I never inconvenience anyone), I take a deep breath and sigh it out.

I used to feel that I was slow in hitting my stride. But slow compared to what? Any woman's development of compassion for her difficulties, confidence in her strengths, and appreciation of her own beauty are significant accomplishments, no matter how lengthy the evolution.

---

36 Victoria Castle, *The Trance of Scarcity: Stop Holding Your Breath and Start Living Your Life* (Sagacious Press, 2007).

"A life's work is always unfinished and requires creativity till the day a person dies. Even If you've managed major accomplishments throughout your life and don't need a model for making a mark, you do need one for enriching an ongoing existence."—Molly Peacock

My dreams reveal my transition from tight to looser garments:

I am supposed to give directions to land a plane and then to translate an encyclopedia.

My overpacked car has no room for me.

By desperately concentrating on it, I am trying to make grass grow faster.

Looking everywhere for my office, I find it inside of me.

A "forgive" function appears on my keyboard.

I am leading a retreat, which is going well despite the monkeys streaming from a mound in the center of the floor.

I am relaxing in the backseat of a self-driving car.

I'm walking in muddy woods, but my shoes are not getting dirty; heavenly music is coming from above, and I stop to listen.

OF MY FATHER'S LOVE

Lately, with daily headache and some accumulated loneliness, and while struggling to finish this book, I have received infusions of Dad's presence. When the grace and power of a circling redtail hawk recently transfixed me, it was as if Dad and I were sharing this experience. This strengthening arrived when I could most use it, as I bring to a finish this work of a lifetime, which has from the beginning felt as if it were being shaped by the writerly, slow hand of God.

It is said that you don't get more out of life than you expect. My experience has been the opposite.

And so, in the biggest surprise of my life, I also dedicate this book to my dad, Orville Wetzel.

Dad with his first catch out of a pond he engineered.

A Bow

My brain stood up and deeply bowed.
"Whoopee," hoorayed my inner crowd.
As this had never happened before
my skeptic's going, "Whoa, girl, whoa."
But budding writer's hot to crow
hair blowing at my mental prow
face forward with a furrowed brow
uncertain where I want to go.

LIBRARY

"How could these makers of so many books that have given so much to my life—how could they possibly be strangers?"—Mary Oliver

I bow in gratitude to these teachers:

ON WRITING

Chabon, Michael: *Bookends: Collected Intros and Outros,* 2019.

Daniell, Rosemary: *The Woman Who Spilled Words All Over Herself,* 1997.

Dobyns, Stephen: *Best Words, Best Order: Essays on Poetry,* 1997; *Next Word, Better Word: The Craft of Writing Poetry,* 2011.

Glück, Louise: *American Originality: Essays on Poetry,* 2022; *Proofs and Theories: Essays on Poetry,* 1994.

Heilbrun, Carolyn: *Writing a Woman's Life,* 1988.

Hirsch, Edward: *100 Poems to Break Your Heart,* 2023; *The Heart of American Poetry,* 2022.

Hirshfield, Jane: *Ten Windows: How Great Poems Transform the World,* 2017; *Nine Gates: Entering the Mind of Poetry, Essays,* 1998.

Housden, Roger: *Ten Poems to Change Your Life,* 2001.

Karr, Mary: *The Art of Memoir,* 2016.

Oliver, Mary: *Upstream: Selected Essays,* 2016; *A Poetry Handbook,* 1994.

Rosen, Kim: *Saved by a Poem: The Transformative Power of Words,* 2009.

Ryan, Kay: *Synthesizing Gravity: Selected Prose,* 2020.

Solnit, Rebecca: *Men Explain Things to Me,* 2014.

Tenen, Dennis Yi: *Literary Theory for Robots: How Computers Learned to Write,* 2024.

Ueland, Brenda: *If You Want to Write,* 2011.

ON CREATIVITY

Alsadir, Nuar: *Animal Joy: A Book of Laughter and Resuscitation*, 2022.

Bechdel, Alison: *The Secret to Superhuman Strength*, 2021.

Berger, John: *Ways of Seeing*, 1973.

Bloom, Harold: *The Daemon Knows: Literary Greatness and the American Sublime*, 2016.

Bringley, Patrick: *All the Beauty in the World: The Metropolitan Museum of Art and Me*, 2023.

Buehrens, John: *Conflagration: How the Transcendentalists Sparked the American Struggle for Racial, Gender, and Social Justice*, 2020.

Cave, Nick, and Sean O'Hagan: *Faith, Hope, and Carnage*, 2022.

Cumming, Laura: *Thunderclap: A Memoir of Art and Life and Sudden Death*, 2023.

Davenport, Guy: *The Geography of the Imagination: Forty Essays*, 1997.

Dederer, Claire: *Monsters: A Fan's Dilemma*, 2023.

Deresiewicz, William: *The Death of the Artist: How Creators Are Struggling to Survive in the Age of Billionaires and Big Tech*, 2020.

Dillon, Brian: *Affinities: On Art and Fascination*, 2023.

Doty, Mark: *Still Life with Oysters and Lemon: On Objects and Intimacy*, 2001; *Art of Description: World into Word*, 2010; *What Is the Grass? Walt Whitman in My Life*, 2021.

Esplund, Lance: *The Art of Looking: How to Read Modern and Contemporary Art*, 2018.

Hughes, Robert: *Nothing if Not Critical: Selected Essays on Art and Artists*, 1992; *American Visions: The Epic History of Art in America*, 1997; *The Shock of the New: The Hundred-Year History of Modern Art*, 2013.

Hustvedt, Siri: *Living, Thinking, Looking: Essays*, 2012; *A Woman Looking at Men Looking at Women: Essays on Art, Sex, and the Mind*, 2016.

Hyde, Lewis: *The Gift: Creativity and the Artist in the Modern World*, 2007; *A Primer for Forgetting: Getting Past the Past*, 2019.

Mann, Sally: *Hold Still: A Memoir with Photographs*, 2016.

Miller, Jean Baker: *Toward a New Psychology of Women*, 1987.

Palmer, Parker: *A Hidden Wholeness: The Journey Toward an Undivided Life*, 2009.

Plotkin, Bill: *Soulcraft: Crossing into the Mysteries of Nature and Psyche*, 2003.

Reed, Arden: *Slow Art: The Experience of Looking, Sacred Images to James Turrell*, 2017.

Rubin, Rick: *The Creative Act: A Way of Being*, 2023.

Saunders, George: *A Swim in a Pond in the Rain: In Which Four Russians Give a Master Class on Writing, Reading, and Life*, 2022.

Scott, A.O.: *Better Living through Criticism: How to Think about Art, Pleasure, Beauty, and Truth,* 2017.

Solnit, Rebecca: *Reflections of My Nonexistence,* 2020.

Winterson, Jeanette: *Art Objects: Essays on Ecstasy and Effrontery,* 1996.

ON GOD

Armstrong, Karen: *A History of God: The 4,000-Year Quest of Judaism, Christianity, and Islam,* 1994; *Twelve Steps to a Compassionate Life,* 2011; *A Short History of Myth,* 2006; *The Lost Art of Scripture: Rescuing the Sacred Texts,* 2020.

Borg, Marcus: *Meeting Jesus Again for the First Time,* 1994.

Boyle, Gregory: *Tattoos on the Heart: The Power of Boundless Compassion,* 2010.

Buechner, Frederick: *Now and Then: A Memoir of Vocation,* 1991; *The Eyes of the Heart: A Memoir of the Lost and Found,* 2000.

Chödrön, Pema: *The Places That Scare You: A Guide to Fearlessness in Difficult Times,* 2001; *When Things Fall Apart: Heart Advice for Difficult Times,* 1997.

de Chardin, Pierre Teilhard: *The Divine Milieu,* 1960.

de Waal, Esther: *Living with Contradictions: An Introduction to Benedictine Spirituality,* 1997.

Dillard, Annie: *For the Time Being,* 1999.

Epstein, Mark: *The Trauma of Everyday Life,* 2014; *Thoughts Without a Thinker: Psychotherapy from a Buddhist Perspective,* 2013.

Feldman, Christina: *Silence: How to Find Inner Peace in a Busy World,* 2001.

Fox, Matthew: *A Spirituality Named Compassion,* 1979; *Original Blessing,* 1983.

Goldstein, Joseph, and Jack Kornfield: *Seeking the Heart of Wisdom: The Path of Insight Meditation,* 2001.

Hanh, Thich Nhat: *Touching Peace: Practicing the Art of Mindful Living,* 2009. (Or any of his work.)

Keating, Thomas: *Intimacy with God,* 1996.

Kongtrul, Dzigar: *It's Up to You: The Practice of Self-Reflection on the Buddhist Path,* 2006; *Light Comes Through: Buddhist Teachings on Awakening to Our Natural Intelligence,* 2009.

Lamott, Anne: *Help, Thanks, Wow: The Three Essential Prayers,* 2012; *Traveling Mercies: Some Thoughts on Faith,* 2000.

May, Gerald: *Addiction and Grace: Love and Spirituality in the Healing of Addictions,* 2017.

McQuiston, John: *Always We Begin Again: The Benedictine Way of Living,* 2001.

Mitchell, Stephen: *The Gospel according to Jesus,* 1994.

Muller, Wayne: *A Life of Being, Having, and Doing Enough,* 2010.

Nouwen, Henri: *Inner Voice of Love: A Journey Through Anguish to Freedom,* 1999; *Finding My Way Home: Pathways to Life and the Spirit,* 2004.

O'Donohue, John: *Walking in Wonder: Eternal Wisdom for a Modern World,* 2015; *Eternal Echoes: Celtic Reflections on Our Yearning to Belong,* 2000; *Anam Cara: Spiritual Wisdom from the Celtic World,* 1999; *To Bless the Space between Us: A Book of Blessings,* 2008.

Ó Tuama, Pádraig: *In the Shelter: Finding a Home in the World,* 2016; *Poetry Unbound: 50 Poems to Open Your World,* 2023.

Richardson, Robert: *Emerson: The Mind on Fire,* 1996.

Rinpoche, Phakchok: *Awakening Dignity,* 2022.

Riso, Don Richard: *The Wisdom of the Enneagram: The Complete Guide to Psychological and Spiritual Growth for the Nine Personality Types,* 1999.

Robinson, Marilynne: *When I Was a Child I Read Books: Essays,* 2012.

Rohr, Richard: *Falling Upward: A Spirituality for the Two Halves of Life,* 2011; *Breathing under Water: Spirituality and the Twelve Steps,* 2021; *Eager to Love: The Alternative Way of Francis of Assisi,* 2014.

Salzberg, Sharon. *Lovingkindness: The Revolutionary Art of Happiness,* 2004.

Smith, Huston: *Forgotten Truth: The Common Vision of the World's Religions,* 1992.

Tan, Chade-Meng: *Search Inside Yourself,* 2012.

Theise, Neil: *Notes on Complexity: A Scientific Theory of Connection, Consciousness, and Being,* 2023.

Tolle, Eckhart: *Power of Now: A Guide to Spiritual Enlightenment,* 2004.

Wiman, Christian: *My Bright Abyss: Meditation of a Modern Believer,* 2014.

Wright, Robert: *Nonzero: The Logic of Human Destiny,* 2000; *The Evolution of God: The Origin of Our Beliefs,* 2010.

Zaleski, Philip, editor: *The Best American Spiritual Writing,* 2006.

Zukav, Gary: *The Seat of the Soul,* 2014.

ON NATURE

Ackerman, Jennifer: *What an Owl Knows: The New Science of the World's Most Enigmatic Birds,* 2023; *The Bird Way: A New Look at How Birds Talk, Work, Play, Parent, and Think,* 2021.

Egginton, William: *The Rigor of Angels: Borges, Heisenberg, Kant, and the Ultimate Nature of Reality,* 2024.

Eiseley, Loren: *The Unexpected Universe,* 1969.

Heinrich, Bernd: *One Man's Owl,* 1987; *A Year in the Maine Woods,* 1995; *The Snoring Bird,* 2007; *One Wild Bird at a Time: Portraits of Individual Lives,* 2017.

Kimmerer, Robin Wall: *Braiding Sweetgrass: Indigenous Wisdom, Scientific Knowledge, and the Teachings of Plants,* 2020.

Kroodsma, Donald: *Birdsong by the Seasons,* 2009; *The Singing Life of Birds,* 2005.

Lopez, Barry: *Crossing Open Ground,* 1989.

Macfarlane, Robert: *The Old Ways: A Journey on Foot,* 2013.

Rothenberg, David: *Survival of the Beautiful: Art, Science, and Evolution,* 2011; *Why Birds Sing: A Journey through the Mystery of Birdsong,* 2005; *Bug Music: How Insects Gave Us Rhythm and Noise,* 2013.

Skutch, Alexander: *The Minds of Birds,* 1996.

Solnit, Rebecca: *The Faraway Nearby,* 2013; *A Field Guide to Getting Lost,* 2006; *Wanderlust: A History of Walking,* 2001.

Stuart-Smith, Sue: *The Well-gardened Mind: The Restorative Power of Nature,* 2020.

Thoreau, Henry David: *Walden,* 1854; *The Maine Woods,* 1864.

Walls, Laura: *Henry David Thoreau: A Life,* 2018.

Weidensaul, Scott: *Living on the Wind: Across the Hemisphere with Migratory Birds,* 1999.

Williams, Terry Tempest: *Refuge: An Unnatural History of Family and Place,* 1992.

Wilson, Edward O.: *Consilience: The Unity of Knowledge,* 1999.

Yong, Ed: *An Immense World: How Animal Senses Reveal Hidden Realms,* 2023; *I Contain Multitudes: The Microbes within Us and a Grander View of Life,* 2018.

WE'RE PUT HERE TO LOVE

THANKS

The most inadequate page of all.

To my *Bill*: I hit the jackpot—my first and only love and lifelong companion who not only makes me laugh but also now takes care of shopping, home furnishing and maintenance, finances, taxes, car, computers, utilities, travel planning, as well as serving as a none-better, all-purpose yardman—who is also a way-too-humble graphic designer and photographer, a four-decade award-winning group home volunteer, and a brother, uncle, great-uncle and godparent revered for his wacky sense of humor as applied to games and to the design of mordant holiday cards.

To my sister *Linda Shantz* and brother *Brian Wetzel*: For your lifelong kindnesses to me and our whole family and for supplying Bill and me with a loving bunch of nieces and nephews and now their beautiful children.

To *Dru Delong*: For your ready ear, steady faith in me, and infallible instincts sorting good poems from bad.

To *Martha S. Taylor*, *Al Bradford*, and *Miriam Shuchman*: For the many times your feedback lit my way forward.

To *Kathryn Kaplan*, *Arnold Rabson*, *Niki Steckler*, and *Penny Williamson*: For your long and enthusiastic support.

To *Kathy Amberger, Deb Ayres, Arlene Balkansky, Emelia Benjamin, Wells Burgess, Donna Chen, Linda Clever, Liz Donnelly, Ellen Feaver, Marian Fetter, Deb German, Sharon Griswold, Margaret Gregory, Mary Guerrera, Sharon Hostler, Molly Houston, Sarah Houston, Yena Hwang, Karla Jutzi, Adina Kalet, Megan Klose, Peg Kroll, Diane Magrane, Renee Marshall, Gayle Monkenon, Christine Petersen, Patty Phillips, Elaine*

Porter, Diane Rawlins, Pat Scheel, Linda Stahl, Trish Stefanik, Mark Stein, Alexandra Suchman, Tony Suchman, Nancy Swift, Kim Theodore, Gretchen Wells, Lois Weik, and *Mimi Zinniel*: For your confidence-boosting observations and your examples of kindness and courage.

To my poetry teachers, *Indran Amirthanayagam, Claudia Gary*, and *Sue Ellen Thompson*, and to my poetry group members, *Lisa Guedea Carreno, Martin Dickens, Tracy Downing, Pamela Levitt*, and *Radhika Yeddanapudi*: For your improvement-facilitating reflections on my poems.

And to all who serve and work for funding for Fairfax County Public Library and Mary Riley Styles Public Library: For enabling my traveling, questing, and gathering from across the ages and the world.

To *Bethany Kelly*, my superb publishing partner, and my godsend of an editor, *Anaik Alcasas*.

And to everyone who's ever encouraged me!

ABOUT THE AUTHOR

Janet Bickel is a nationally recognized career and leadership development expert with 50 years of experience in academic medicine and
science. Over 125 academic health centers and 35 professional societies
have invited her presentations and consultations. During the 25 years
prior to creating her own coaching business, Janet held positions of
increasing leadership at the Association of American Medical Colleges,
where she established an influential Office of Women in Medicine
and Science. Her publications include over 60 peer-reviewed articles,
numerous commentaries, and three books: *Equip Your Inner Coach:
Personal, Career, and Leadership Development in an Uncertain Age*
(2022), *Women in Medicine: Getting In, Growing, and Advancing* (2000),
and *Educating for Professionalism: Creating a Culture of Humanism in
Medical Education* (with Delese Wear, 2000). https://janetbickel.com

WE'RE PUT HERE TO LOVE